The John Clare Society Journal

The official Journal of the John Clare Society,
published annually to reflect the interest in, and approaches to,
the life and work of the poet John Clare.

Editor
Simon Kövesi
(University of Glasgow)

Reviews Editor
Erin Lafford
(West Midlands Institute of Psychotherapy)

Advisory Board
Jonathan Bate (Arizona State University)
Gerard Carruthers (University of Glasgow)
Katey Castellano (James Madison University)
Paul Chirico (Fitzwilliam College, Cambridge)
Johanne Clare (George Brown College, Toronto)
Richard Cronin (University of Glasgow)
Paul Farley (Lancaster University)
John Gardner (Anglia Ruskin University)
John Goodridge (Nottingham Trent University)
Nick Groom (University of Macau)
Robert Heyes (John Clare Society)
Andrew Hodgson (University of Birmingham)
C. M. Jackson-Houlston (Oxford Brookes University)
Bridget Keegan (Creighton University, Omaha)
Peter Kitson (University of East Anglia)
Donna Landry (University of Kent)
Francesca Mackenney (Manchester Metropolitan University)
Emma Mason (University of Warwick)
Scott McEathron (Southern Illinois University)
James McKusick (University of Missouri–Kansas City)
Nicholas Roe (University of St Andrews)
Adam Rounce (University of Nottingham)
Fiona Stafford (Somerville College, Oxford)
Sarah Zimmerman (Fordham University)

Number 44   July 2025

The John Clare Society

Patron: Richard Mabey

President: John Goodridge

Vice Presidents: Peter Cox, Rodney Lines, Kelsey Thornton

Chair: Sue Holgate

Vice-Chair, Festival Organiser and Publicity Officer: Ann Marshall

Hon. Sectretary: Karen Lakey

Hon. Treasurer and Sales Officer: David Smith

Journal Editor: Simon Kövesi

Newsletter Editor: Stephen Sullivan

Archivist: Sam Ward

Membership Secretary: Valerie Pedlar

Committee Members: Anna Kinnaird, Mike Mecham and Jonathan Wonham

North American Representative: James McKusick

The John Clare Society is a UK Registered Charity, number 1124846

New members are always welcome; please contact Dr Valerie Pedlar, 20 Delamere Road, Ainsdale, Southport, PR8 2RD
Email: vpedlar@yahoo.co.uk

For journal submission details, please contact the Editor:
Professor Simon Kövesi, School of Critical Studies,
5, University Gardens (Room 304),
University of Glasgow, G12 8QH, Scotland, simon.kovesi@glasgow.ac.uk

© 2025 published by the John Clare Society
Printed by: Joshua Horgan, Unit 2, Glenmore Business Centre, Witney,
Oxon, OX29 0AA
www.joshuahorgan.co.uk

Typesetting by: www.ratherfinedesign.co.uk

ISBN 978-1-9161355-8-1

This is a limited edition of 500, free to full members of the Society,
£7.00 if purchased separately.

Contents

EDITORIAL	4
NO SEX PLEASE, WE'RE EDITORS *Robert Heyes*	5

'ITCHING AFTER RYHME': THE PSYCHOPHYSIOLOGICAL
    FUNCTION OF ITCH IN JOHN CLARE'S WRITING
        Catherine McNally
	13

I AM! AGAIN *Mark Fiddes*	31

'AND SOON THE WISPER WENT ABOUT THE TOWN': GOSSIPS
    AND GOSSIPING IN JOHN CLARE'S NARRATIVE POETRY
        Emlyn David
	33

JOHN CLARE AND THE SHIFTING SKYLARK *Sam Hickford and Em Challinor*	51
REVIEWS	67
CONTRIBUTORS	78
ABBREVIATIONS	80

Editorial

We are lucky to feature the contributions of two leading artists: Mark Fiddes is an award-winning poet with a lifelong connection to Clare. For the contribution of this year's front-cover art warm thanks are due to Charlotte Strawbridge, who allowed us to reproduce her oil painting entitled 'Bombus'. My thanks also to James Keech, Archivist at Peterborough Archives Service, for handling the reproduction on p. 7. It's so important to understand the wild variety of pleasures and problems Clare's texts present, and there's no better way to do that than looking at one of Clare's handwritten manuscripts.

All three books advertised on our colour cover pages have direct connections to this journal – Nic Wilson and John Goodridge have published here – while the highly significant collection *Cambridge Companion to John Clare* features many contributors who have published here too. Readers can access a generous discount from Cambridge University Press via the code in the advert, while David Stewart in the reviews section assesses the collection for us too. Readers should also note the latest Clare selection to be published by this society – *Clare's People*, edited by Mike Mecham – just in print and advertised on p. 12. These are lively and exciting times in the rich history of books about the poet. Our annual bibliography will prove that, when it returns next year.

My thanks to a wide variety of anonymous referees this year, all of whom work generously and for free, offering their world-leading academic expertise to ensure our publication maintains the high standards set by our predecessor editors, supporting authors on the journey to publication, while also keeping the journal as accessible and open as possible. I've been editing this journal since 2008, and the job has been the privilege of my working life. I love doing it, but it is high time for me to find someone else to take it on, so that the study and celebration of Clare can continue to grow, renew and expand. If you are interested, please do get in touch.

Simon Kövesi
University of Glasgow

No Sex Please, We're Editors
Robert Heyes

Over the years there has not been a great deal of discussion of John Clare's use of dialect words, and when this topic has been mentioned there is one obvious and simple fact which tends to be overlooked, namely that for much of the time the young Clare would not have realised that he was using dialect words, or provincialisms as they were known two centuries ago. I'm in my eighties, but there are words I know, and sometimes use, whose status is a mystery to me. Are they Lincolnshire words I learned as a child? Are they Lancashire words I picked up from my father or his relatives? Or are they words which are in common use? I really don't know.

How much more difficult it would have been for Clare, at the beginning of his career as a writer, when his acquaintance was largely restricted to his fellow villagers and, although he had embarked on a programme of self-improvement, his reading was necessarily limited. His first two books, *Poems, Descriptive of Rural Life and Scenery* (1820) and *The Village Minstrel, and Other Poems* (1821), both had glossaries at the end to explain the meaning of the provincialisms found in the poems. By the time Clare's final two volumes, *The Shepherd's Calendar* (1827) and *The Rural Muse* (1835), were published a glossary was no longer required; Clare's wider acquaintance, and wider reading, had clarified his mind on this matter.

The inclusion of dialect words might not necessarily have been detrimental to a work. It would not have been obvious at the time, but the 1820s saw the beginning of a serious interest in provincialisms. Among the books on the subject published in that decade were Moor's *Suffolk Words and Phrases*, Carr's *Craven Dialect*, Brockett's *Glossary of North Country Words*, Jennings's *Somersetshire Dialect*, Wilbraham's *Cheshire Glossary*, Hunter's *Hallamshire Glossary* and Forby's *Vocabulary of East Anglia*.[1] Many other similar works were published in the years that followed, of which Anne Elizabeth Baker's *Glossary of Northamptonshire Words and Phrases* was a typical example.[2] Clare is known to have helped Miss Baker with this work; I remember a bookseller once cataloguing a copy and describing it as John Clare's fifth book – ambitious, but a little exaggerated. However, it is certainly true that the book contains not only extracts from Clare's published works illustrating the usage of dialect words, but also lines from his manuscript poetry which have not survived elsewhere.[3]

One of the weaknesses of such books is that dialect and county boundaries do not coincide. The words in Miss Baker's *Glossary* were, no doubt, used in Northamptonshire, but they were not used all over the county. Dialect words could, indeed, be confined to a surprisingly small area. I recall a story told by a former colleague of mine, who grew up in a village in north Yorkshire where she attended the village school. One day a family moved into the village from another village, three miles away. There was a little boy in the family, who turned up at the school – and nobody could understand him. *Three miles!* John Clare's dialect is far more likely to have resembled the language of south Lincolnshire, only a very few miles to the north, than the dialect of the other end of Northamptonshire, sixty or seventy miles distant. Indeed, he uses words and phrases which I recognise from my Lincolnshire childhood, in what was then Kesteven.

Ten or a dozen years ago I bumped into Professor Eric Robinson at the John Clare Festival. He told me that he had become increasingly dissatisfied with the glossaries appended to his editions of Clare's poems, although these are the most comprehensive glossaries we have. He was working on a new glossary using the resources of the Folger Shakespeare Library in Washington D. C., which was readily accessible from his home in Virginia. Unfortunately, his death meant that this work was never completed, but there is a desperate need for it, and an opportunity for a scholar of a lexicographical bent.

I want to look at a couple of poems where a failure to understand Clare's language has led to mistakes and misunderstandings. One is the poem usually known as 'The Mouse's Nest', although Clare himself did not give the poem a title; there is only one manuscript of the poem, which is in the John Clare Collection in Peterborough Central Library:

> I found a ball of grass among the hay
> & proged it as I passed & went away
> & when I looked I fancied somthing stirred
> & turned agen & hoped to catch the bird
> When out an old mouse bolted in the wheat
> With all her young ones hanging at her teats

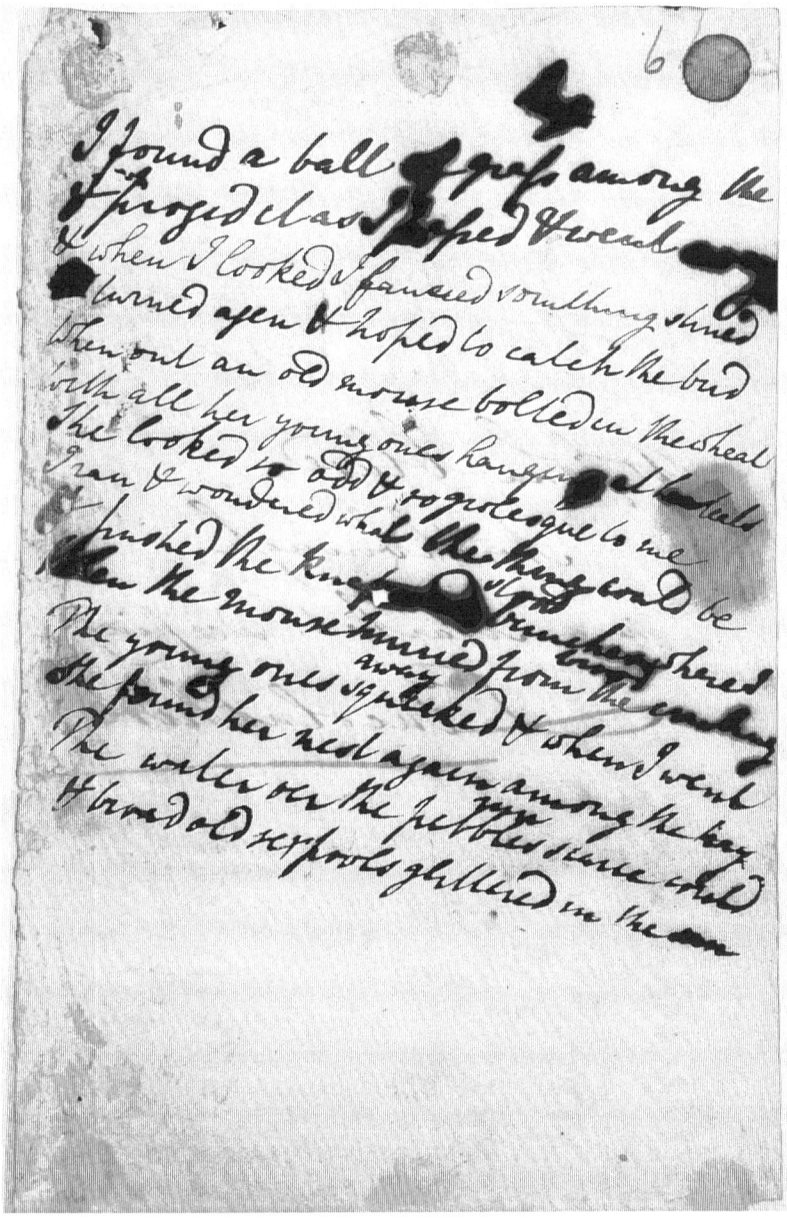

Image of John Clare Manuscript MS A61, page 6. Publication rights obtained from Peterborough Archives Service.

> She looked so odd & so grotesque to me
> I ran & wondered what the thing could be
> & pushed the knapweed bunches where I stood
> When the mouse hurried from the crawling brood
> The young ones squeaked & when I went away
> She found her nest again among the hay
> The water oer the pebbles scarce could run
> & broad old sexpools glittered in the sun[4]

This poem was first published by John and Anne Tibble in their two-volume edition of Clare's poetry in 1935, a much fuller selection than any that had previously been available. In their version 'sexpools' in the last line had disappeared, being replaced by 'cesspools'. John Clare had clearly written 'sexpools' and the Tibbles gave no indication of what they had done, nor did they offer any explanation of what 'cesspools' might be.[5] The modern meaning is a tank or receptacle of some sort for the storage of waste water or sewage, not a very poetic subject.

Subsequent twentieth-century editions of Clare's poetry followed the Tibbles' lead. Geoffrey Grigson's *Selected Poems* of 1950, the Tibbles' own selection for Everyman's Library in 1965, Raymond and Merryn Williams's 1986 selection of the poetry and prose and the Oxford World's Classics edition of the Major Works in 1984 all had 'cesspools', without ever explaining the meaning of the word.[6] Of course, it is anybody's guess just how many of these editors had actually been to Peterborough to look at the manuscript of the poem; one suspects that some of them simply copied what the Tibbles wrote, and had no more idea than the rest of us that the text had been tampered with.

It was sixty years after the first publication of the poem that the word 'sexpools' eventually appeared in print. This was in *Northborough Sonnets*, edited by Eric Robinson, David Powell and P. M. S. Dawson. However, the poem still contained the word 'cesspools', but in the notes to the volume we are told that this 'is an editorial emendation from Clare's "sexpools"'. So, progress of a sort, but we still aren't told what 'cesspools' means.[7]

It was in 2003 that the poem finally appeared as Clare had written it, in the fifth and final volume of *Poems of the Middle Period*, from the Clarendon Press. Here, if we look up 'sexpools' in the glossary, we find – you guessed it – 'see cesspools'. Cesspools is defined as 'water which gathers on the "cess" or land between a river and its bank when the river is low'.[8] This meaning is found in one or two nineteenth-century glossaries, and it has a certain plausibility. The preceding line of the poem refers to a river or stream which has little water in it, so there would have been space between the water and the bank. But would any pools which formed there be 'broad' and 'old'? It seems unlikely.

Also in 2003 came Jonathan Bate's selection of Clare's poetry and this, too, printed 'sexpools' in the final line. In the glossary Professor Bate described 'sexpools' as 'rainwater pools in areas where peat has been dug out'.[9] No source is given for this, but it seems a much more likely explanation of Clare's word. The digging of peat has a long history in the Fenland, providing fuel in an area where it was otherwise scarce, and the Clares were among the families who used it. Edward Drury, giving his cousin John Taylor, on 26 April 1819, an account of his first visit to Clare's cottage in Helpston, mentioned that 'they were sitting against a little bit of a fire of sods & stick'.[10] 'Sod' is one of those words whose currency I am unsure of, but it is simply another word for a piece of turf.

A century earlier, in 1712, the Revd John Morton, in *The Natural History of Northamptonshire*, devotes considerable space to the extraction of peat. Always referred to locally as turf, it was dug up in pieces the size and shape of a brick; Morton refers to the pieces of turf, as 'sesses'.[11] More recent works call them cesses,[12] but of course dialect words belong to an oral, not a written culture, they are spoken, not written down. If the need arises to write them there is no correct way to spell them, the writer must be guided by the sound of the word. This is obviously what Clare was doing with 'sexpools'. What we can't know, of course, is exactly what word was used for turf in Helpston or, more importantly, how it was pronounced.

The adjectives 'broad' and 'old' in the last line of the poem, describing the 'sexpools', would be appropriate here. The layers of peat were never more than a few feet thick; according to John Morton they were 'in some Places six Foot, in others scarcely one'.[13] The workings left behind would therefore be wide but shallow, they might well be old and, having filled up with water, they would indeed glitter in the summer sun. Professor Sir Harry Godwin wrote, in 1978, that '[a]t my own earliest visit to Wicken I recall that a large part of Adventurers' Fen was crossed by peat diggers' trenches that were all water-filled'.[14] In 1712 John Morton remarked that: 'In the Months of *April* and *May*, there is always Water in the Turfe-pits. Nay in *August*, in a dry Summer, I have observ'd Water there.'[15]

There is another Clare poem where people have been misled by failure to understand a dialect word; this is 'The Mores', a lengthy poem which begins:

> Far spread the moorey ground a level scene
> Bespread with rush & one eternal green
> That never felt the rage of blundering plough
> Though centurys wreathed spring blossoms on its brow
> Still meeting plains that stretched them far away
> In uncheckt shadows of green brown & grey
> Unbounded freedom ruled the wandering scene
> Nor fence of ownership crept in between
> To hide the prospect of the following eye
> Its only bondage was the circling sky
> One mighty flat undwarfed by bush & tree
> Spread its faint shadow of immensity
> & lost itself which seemed to eke its bounds
> In the blue mist the orisons edge surrounds[16]

In so far as critics have thought about what 'mores' or 'moors' we are talking about (which isn't far) they seem to have assumed that 'moor' meant then what it means now. Moor nowadays is used to refer to upland areas, usually bleak and windswept, such as Dartmoor and Exmoor in the south-west of England and, in the north, the Pennine moors, the Lake District and the North York Moors. These are clearly many miles away, literally and metaphorically, from the countryside with which Clare was familiar.

It is obvious from these first few lines of the poem that we are in the Fens; we are, in fact, in the peat lands; moor is defined as: 'The Fenland name for peat. Peat moors'.[17] Morton refers to 'moory ground', 'moory land', and 'moory common',[18] and the word survives in place names such as Wildmore Fen.

It is important, therefore, when reading Clare's poetry and prose, to always remember that the words he uses may have a meaning beyond the obvious one. Dialect words may be the same as words with which we are familiar, but have quite a different meaning. We await an adequate glossary which would explain these terms.

NOTES

1. Edward Moor, *Suffolk Words and Phrases, or, an Attempt to Collect the Lingual Localisms of that County* (Woodbridge: Printed by J. Loder for R. Hunter, 1823); [William Carr] *Horae Momenta Cravenae, or, The Craven Dialect Exemplified in Two Dialogues, Between Farmer Giles and His Neighbour Bridget, To Which is Annexed a Copious Glossary, by a Native of Craven* (London: Hurst, Robinson, 1824); John Trotter Brockett, *A Glossary of North Country Words, In Use* (Newcastle upon Tyne: Printed by T. and J. Hodgson, for E. Charnley, 1825); James Jennings, *Observations On Some of the Dialects in the West of England, Particularly Somersetshire: with a Glossary of Words Now in Use There; and Poems and other Pieces, Exemplifying the Dialect* (London: Baldwin, Cradock, and Joy, 1825); Roger Wilbraham, *An Attempt at a Glossary of Some Words Used in Cheshire* (London: T. Rodd, 1826); Joseph Hunter, *The Hallamshire Glossary* (London: William Pickering, 1829); Robert Forby, *The Vocabulary of East Anglia; an Attempt to Record the Vulgar Tongue of the Twin Sister Counties, Norfolk and Suffolk, as it Existed in the Last Twenty Years of the Eighteenth Century, and Still Exists* (London: J. B. Nichols and Son, 1830).
2. Anne Elizabeth Baker, *Glossary of Northamptonshire Words and Phrases, with Examples of their Colloquial Use, and Illustrations from Various Authors: to which are added, the Customs of the County*, 2 vols (London: John Russell Smith, and Northampton: Abel & Sons, and Mark Dorman, 1854).
3. *Later Poems*, II, pp. 1107-13.
4. *Middle Period*, V, p. 246.
5. *The Poems of John Clare*, ed. by J. W. Tibble, 2 vols (London: Dent, 1935), p. 370.
6. *Selected Poems of John Clare*, ed. by Geoffrey Grigson (London: Routledge and Kegan Paul, 1950), p. 173; *John Clare: Selected Poems*, ed. by J. W. Tibble and Anne Tibble (London: Dent, 1965), p. 234; *John Clare: Selected Poetry and Prose*, ed. by Merryn and Raymond Williams (London: Methuen, 1986), p. 154; *John Clare: Major Works*, ed. by Eric Robinson and David Powell (Oxford: Oxford University Press, 1984), p. 263.
7. John Clare, *Northborough Sonnets*, ed. by Eric Robinson, David Powell and P.M.S. Dawson (Ashington: Carcanet, 1995), pp. 54, 116.
8. *Middle Period*, V, pp. 246, 694, 655.
9. *John Clare: Selected Poems*, ed. by Jonathan Bate (London: Faber, 2003), pp. 228, 306.
10. Northampton Public Library, John Clare Collection, Manuscript 43(2).
11. John Morton, *The Natural History of Northamptonshire* (London: R. Knaplock and R. Wilkin, 1712), p. 86.
12. Hilary Healey, *A Fenland Landscape Glossary for Lincolnshire* (Lincoln: Lincolnshire Books, 1997), p. 7.
13. Morton, p. 85.
14. Sir Harry Godwin, *Fenland: its Ancient Past and Uncertain Future* (Cambridge: Cambridge University Press, 1978), p. 123. Chapter 12, on 'Peat and its winning', contains much valuable information on the subject.
15. Morton, p. 84.
16. *Middle Period*, II, p. 347.
17. Joan Sims-Kimbrey, *Wodds and Doggerybaw: A Lincolnshire Dialect Dictionary* (Boston: Richard Kay, 1995), p. 195.
18. Morton, pp. 9, 36, 76.

JOHN CLARE SOCIETY

AVAILABLE FROM JULY 2025

Clare's People

A new selection of John Clare's poetry and prose, edited by Mike Mecham, with original illustrations by Petra Wonham and John Bangay

The selection extends Clare's gaze to the people who inhabited his world. Revealing Clare's humanity alongside his sharp social observation, this collection displays the poet's empathy as well as his anger at injustice

Copies of the book, at a special launch price of £12, postage free, can be ordered from the Sales Officer, The John Clare Society, **djsapt@gmail.com**

'Itching after ryhme':
The Psychophysiological Function of Itch in John Clare's Writing

Catherine McNally

In his autobiographical fragments, John Clare expresses irritation towards the vexatious rules of grammar which made him feel 'quite in the suds'; yet, he also recalls his intense motivation and keen ambition to 'try', resolving:

> I had hardly h[e]ard the name of grammer while at school – but as I had an itch for trying at every thing I got hold of I determ[i]ned to try grammer[1]

While Clare's idiosyncratic grammar and appetite for learning have been much documented, scholarship has neglected the curious sensory reaction provoked by Clare's learning and writing, which he describes as an 'itch'.[2] This 'itch' to 'try', conveys the enterprise of an eager autodidact, but is only one example of the many literal and figurative itch sensations Clare records in his writing.[3] Sometimes, the itch expresses simultaneous creative urgency and annoyance, suggesting what galvanises also exhausts. This itch could be so vexatious that Clare hoped his daughter would not be blighted by the compulsion to 'itch at rhymes' and would remain 'unknown to rhyming bother'.[4] If learning and writing causes Clare both literally and figuratively to itch, then his creative process can be understood as a cycle of aggravation and alleviation. Tracking the iterations of itch as a motif throughout Clare's writing reveals how poetry initiates, satisfies, and frequently rekindles the itching sensation that he documents, exponentially amplifying a cycle of discomfort and pleasure. Poetry might be a tribulation, but it also compels: Clare is always 'itching after ryhme'.[5]

To itch is to adjust, regulating the body when it is uncomfortable; a process helpfully elucidated by Charles Rosenburg whose discussion of late nineteenth-century therapeutics, is pertinent here:

One could not live well without food and air and water; one had to live in a particular climate, subject to one's body and to a particular style of life and work. Each of these factors implied a necessary and continuing physiological adjustment. The body was always in a state of becoming – and thus always in jeopardy.[6]

Rosenburg's term 'becoming' encapsulates the two simultaneous and reciprocal aspects of bodily existence: the body must adapt to shifts in the external environment, and respond to cycles of internal desire. For Rosenburg perpetual change and constant danger are mutually contingent, as indicated by the shift from auspicious 'becoming' to ominous 'jeopardy'. Yet the creative potential inherent in a restless precarity eludes Rosenburg. In Clare's writing, the phases of discomfort and pleasure indicated by the 'itch-scratch-itch' cycle represent a body 'becoming', but this does not necessarily place Clare in 'jeopardy', rather, this danger can be creatively generative.[7]

In the following essay I exploit the fluctuations between pain and pleasure, aggravation and alleviation, implied by Rosenburg's term 'becoming', to frame the various itches Clare experiences. I explore the associations that Clare establishes between itching and writing in the context of medical science, and detail how the formal and syntactical elements of Clare's poetry participate in the dynamics of compulsion, vexation, and pleasure. I then position Clare's itching, fevered disposition within the contemporary understanding of hypochondria: a condition informed by the intersection between literary culture and psychophysiology, and exacerbated by Clare's precarious economic situation. Next, I consider Clare's sensitised itching persona as a manifestation of the sublime and explore how anxieties about the creative process are figured as examples of Burkean 'terror' localised in the itching mind and body. Also I argue that finding sublimity on a miniature scale provides, for Clare, momentary respite from the itch of poetic inspiration. Through an examination of his prose, poetry, and letters, I consider the extent to which the rich polysemy of itch reveals how bodily and mental agitation were integral to Clare's unique poetic voice.

Medical science offers an interpretive framework within which Clare's poetic sensibility is revealed as innately pruriceptive. The complex aetiology of an itch encompasses irritation of the pruriceptors in the skin, faults in the nervous system, and additionally manifest as a symptom of mental illness.[8] Afflicted with bouts of ill health, Clare records being haunted by depression and 'blue devils', all of which are rendered figuratively in his poetry and writing as a recurring itch motif.[9] Samuel Johnson's informative definition of prurience (from the Latin *pruris*: to itch), as 'an itching or a great desire or appetite to any thing' figures unchecked aspiration as a persistent itch.[10] Clare's itch is not solely an uncomfortable physiological event, but accords with this understanding of prurience, indeed he confesses to 'itching after everything'; he 'coud not stop [his] thoughts'. Writing was an impulsive activity for Clare, and spurred by this itching appetite for poetry he would spontaneously drop 'down behind a hedge bush or dyke' to scribble drafts of verse.[11] Here the act of writing, which quietens his compulsively itching mind and eases his mental turmoil, involves a physiological adjustment of his whole body.

Whilst writing can ease the unsettled mind, it can simultaneously be a source of torment, and this experience of aggravation and alleviation is particularised as an itching sensation across Clare's prose. In a letter to his publisher John Taylor, Clare justifies his prolixity in terms that reflect Rosenburg's observation of the body's 'continuing physiological adjustment', explicitly articulating this necessary 'adjustment' as an itch to create: 'I can assure you I feel myself a great itching always to trouble you with my scrawl'.[12] Here Clare's 'scrawl' behaves as a pleasurable scratch for the itch of inspiration, and this 'great itching', suggestive of a formidable impulse to compose, reappears in a poem attached to another letter to Taylor, that includes the line 'my pen is often on the itch'.[13] Here, the curiosity and urgency impelling Clare's creative process is exemplified by the itching pen as a metonym for authorial composition. In both examples, the creativity conveyed by the itch motif implies aggravation requiring alleviation. In another letter written to Taylor, Clare disparages William Wordsworth's poems, calling them 'Nursery ryhmes', and commenting that they 'are ridiculous so much so that reading them gives me the itch of parody which I cannot resist – I did one the other day to ease my mind'.[14] The compulsion to write certainly places Clare's body in a state of itching 'jeopardy' – peril that impels poetry. Clare 'cannot resist' assuaging his strikingly itchy physiological reaction to poetic inspiration.

'The Progress of Ryhme' comprehensively demonstrates the various and contradictory uses of the itch motif that Clare employs across his writing. In this poem, his creative process is articulated as a complex cycle in which writing both provokes and eases psychological and physiological aggravation. Poetic inspiration can be a vexation that leaves Clare 'itching after ryhme' in 'silent

'Study of a Right Hand', Benjamin Robert Haydon (1786-1846).
Courtesy National Gallery of Art, Washington.

shame', but is also 'like a friend' through which he expresses delight in the natural world (l. 204; l. 271; l. 29). In the following lines, poetry mitigates discomfort; Clare celebrates liberation from the drudgery of agricultural labour:

> While threshing in the dusty barn
> Or squashing in the ditch to earn
> A pittance that would scarce alow
> One joy to smooth my sweating brow
> Where drop by drop would chace and fall
> – Thy presence triumphed over all (ll. 9-14)

Clare's muscular strain and physical exertion, indicated by the succession of vigorous verbs ('threshing', 'squashing', 'sweating') are eased by the delayed main clause: 'Thy presence triumphed over all'. If a state of itching is a somatic manifestation of the body's essential 'continual physiological adjustment', then poetry provides affective consolation, providing an intellectual *scratch* that alleviates the itch of intense physical exertion associated with Clare's agricultural lifestyle.[15] Michael Nicholson analyses physical, emotional, ecological and political forms of distress as a force that 'universally permeat[es] diverse dynamic systems' in Clare's poetry. While he recognises that 'Clare's poetics of distress participates in an expansive literary tradition of distressed works and lives', by maintaining an understanding of stress as a ubiquitous force Nicholson unpicks how Clare's verse 'incessantly capitalises on the linguistic contingency' of 'terms of affliction [...] and comfort' ('"oppress", "repossess", "press", "depress"' are often rhymed with "rest, "blessed", and "progress"').[16] Comfort and discomfort are mutually contingent, as Nicholson demonstrates, but setting these contraries within the 'itch-scratch-itch' cycle reveals how alleviation can give rise to aggravation.[17]

Paradoxically, distress can be productive, urging the body to adjust to a more comfortable state. 'The Progress of Ryhme' records this adjustment as the daily pressures felt by Clare, as a writer, and as an agricultural labourer, shift between irritation and inspiration, an inherent duality encapsulated by the repetition of 'strain' throughout the poem. The first appearance of 'strain' occurs in the lines: 'I felt that I'd a right to song / & sung – but in a timid strain' (ll. 80-1). As 'but' unexpectedly undercuts the buoyant tone, the jubilant crescendo achieved by the sibilant shift from 'song' to 'sung' is abruptly truncated. Confident singing is muted and becomes a 'timid strain'; a phrase which exploits the musical connotations of 'strain', 'song' and 'sung', but also embroils melody with the concealed exertion Clare experienced in the composition of poetry. As the poem continues, a repeated rhyme between 'strain' and 'again' underscores Clare's persistent effort, and compounds the conflict established within the word 'strain'. While listening to birdsong, Clare explains how he 'caught with eager ear the strain / & sung the music oer again' (ll. 141-2). Later, he imagines 'That musics self had left the sky / To cheer me with its majic strain / & then I hummed the words again' (ll. 264-6). In both instances, Clare exploits the duality of 'strain' so that the word oscillates between exertion and musicality. The effort and frustration that arises from composing 'song' creates semantic indecision as 'strain' continually adjusts in meaning. Consequently, Clare's creative process can be understood as a generative 'itching after ryhme' as individual words adjust and itch, accommodating a myriad of literal and figurative resonances in Clare's 'threshing' and 'squashing' body, in his strained mind, and in his syntax.

Clare's innately pruriceptive style creates the conditions for multiplicity, a state augmented by the repetition of 'still' throughout 'The Progress of Ryhme', which aurally emphasises a sustained ambition to 'sing as well as greater men' (l. 109). Clare admires the constancy of the 'fields & woods' that provide him with poetic inspiration, humbly admitting that:

> if my song be weak or tame
> Tis I not they who bear the blame
> But hope & cheer through good & ill
> They are my aids to worship still
> Still growing [...] (ll. 147-51)

Here the anadiplotic 'still' is restless and paradoxical, denoting *always* (and therefore in motion), and *motionless*, two conditions of the word that are incisively elucidated by Murray Krieger: 'still' movement as quiet, unmoving movement; 'still' moving as a forever-now movement, always in process, un-ending.[18] This 'always in process' quality of 'still' accommodates two frustratingly antagonistic states of being, perpetuity and inertia, which remain as unresolved variables, semantically delineating the persistently troubling 'state of becoming' that Clare's itching, sensitised persona navigates.[19]

Not only are grammar and syntax impacted by the dynamics of an 'itch-scratch-itch' cycle, but the physiological connotations of the vocabulary associated with itching mean that Clare's creative process is described in explicitly physical language as an unavoidable compulsion: he 'felt without a single skill / That instinct that would not be still' (ll. 197-8). This 'instinct' triggers an intense physical response, indicated by Clare's 'heav[ing]' chest, which is compared to his 'breath / That burned & chilled & went & came' (ll. 200-201). The rapidity of the polysyndetic list pulses with feverish symptoms, mimicking an urgent physiological response to poetic inspiration. This adrenaline-fuelled burning and itching, in which poetry finds no linguistic expression, is analogous to the sublime sensation that Sarah Houghton-Walker, when discussing 'The Sublime Vision of John Clare', defines as 'the point at which language breaks down, yet where one feels that there is something to express or communicate'.[20] Later I will fully develop how the sublime catalyses, and sometimes calms, itching sensations. But, for now, it is worth noting that while Clare is galvanised by this unarticulated 'instinct' for poetry, his visceral response to irresistible stimuli negates his sense of agency and leaves him 'itching after ryhme'. Importantly, the temporo-spatial properties of the preposition 'after' are disorientated. 'Itching after ryhme' initially associates the itching sensation with a hankering 'after' creative satisfaction, but the modification 'left me' also positions Clare as 'itching' in a state of frustration, and grappling with anxieties about the inadequacies of his verse. The line complicates this itching: is poetry part of the aetiology or the remedy? Ralf Paus's modern medical assertion that 'it is the brain that itches, not the skin' illuminates Clare's itching in relation to his 'instinct' for poetic composition.[21] In this moment, itching functions psychologically to indicate curiosity, or it functions physiologically as a somatic irritant. These two conflicting aspects of the itch helps elucidate another aspect of Clare's identity: the relationship between his writing and his health.

In the 'Introduction' to Clare's first volume of poetry, *Poems Descriptive of Rural Life and Scenery* (1820), Taylor is alert to the pecuniary and reputational benefits of positioning Clare within a literary culture that made pathology a spectacle. Writing that Clare was 'the least favoured by circumstances, and the most destitute of friends, of any that ever existed', Taylor exploits the popular demand for untutored, impoverished, and melancholic poetic genius.²² George Rousseau, writing on Samuel Taylor Coleridge, identifies how 'the Romantic sickly poet [...] became a type, one with legitimate medical credentials', clarifying how deliberate editorial manoeuvring positioned Clare in a literary culture that understood melancholy as a prerequisite for poetic sensibility.²³ However, for Clare, ill health is not an expedient affectation and his poetic voice is shaped by genuine fears. A particular terror, alluded to in the Sketches, was the potential consequence of sexual indiscretion. He writes that 'not only my health but my life has often been on the eve of its sacrifice by an illness too well known, and to[o] disgusting to mention'.²⁴ Clare was deeply anxious that he had contracted syphilis, as Jonathan Bate notes, 'Dr Nesbitt of the Northampton Asylum told Clare's first biographer that he had always been led to believe that the poet's mental affliction had its "origin in dissipation"'.²⁵ Ambiguously locating the cause of Clare's 'affliction[s]' in 'dissipation', a word that connotes both alcoholic and sexual recklessness, is a tentative diagnosis. Nevertheless, the fear of venereal disease remained a specifically itchy health anxiety for Clare; his 'pen is', tellingly, 'often on the itch'. This salacious pun is unmistakeable. Whether deliberately contrived or unwittingly communicated, the particular inflammatory connotations inherent in pathology, creativity, and pruritus coalesce in Clare's distinctive poetic voice.

In *The Anatomy of Melancholy* (1621), Robert Burton observes that psychological conflict can manifest as corporeal symptoms ('melancholy gets out at the superficies of the skinne'), and identifies one of the 'prognosticks of melancholy' as an 'itch'.²⁶ His observation anticipates modern psychiatric studies which confirm that 'psychogenic factors [anxiety and depression] frequently enhance somatic sensations, such as pruritus or pain'.²⁷ Burton additionally draws a 'connection between hypochondriacal melancholy and mental genius' which manifests particularly in poets and academics.²⁸ Burton's text, which demonstrates what Erin Lafford identifies as a 'slippage' between the terms hypochondria and melancholy, contributed to the fashion for hypochondria, amplifying a trend for melancholy poetics in the eighteenth century. As Lafford argues, 'hypochondria can become a lens through which to consider Clare's lyric subjectivity' even though definitions 'of hypochondria in the period insist almost invariably on a scholastic, sedentary lifestyle as one of its main causes'.²⁹ Clare's hypochondriacal tendency, inflected by Burton's idea of melancholy as an itch, offers a way of understanding psychosomatic itching in relation to his 'lyric subjectivity', one afflicted with itching, prickling, and burning sensations

The psychosomatic conditions of itching are painfully felt and articulated by Clare as he complains to Taylor about the awful 'burning heat in my fundament where the humour again made its appearance with prickly pains in head arms & shoulders', a state that leaves him 'alarmed & anxious to get better'.[30] Whilst Clare's distress over his unruly, intemperate body aligns with a modern definition of hypochondria as 'somatic amplification disorder',[31] in the Eighteenth Century diagnoses of hypochondria frequently oscillated between psychological and physiological interpretations. In this letter, Clare's distinctly medicalised vocabulary, 'burning' and 'prickly', suggests an aggravating itch indicating an inflamed physiology, one that causes him extreme psychological 'alarm'. Yet, as 'An Effusion to Poetry' demonstrates, this 'alarm' can be relieved by poetry: 'When on pillowd thorns I weep [...] Then thou charm from heaven above / Comfort's cordial dost thou prove'.[32] For Clare, poetry remedies his distressed body and is the medicinal 'cordial' that relieves him from the sharp discomfort conveyed by the oxymoron 'pillowd thorns', and additionally from a vexatious cycle of aggravation and alleviation. To read this poem within the narrow Romantic convention for staging 'ill, languorous, hypersensitive' bodies that G. Rousseau identifies as the 'principal characteristic of the Romantic sensibility' is limiting.[33] Situated in the wider context of Clare's itch motif, 'An Effusion to Poetry', with its intent to remedy the distressed body with poetry, complicates the extent to which Clare's early poems can be considered solely as hypochondriacal or melancholic artifice: they enmesh distinctly pathological personal experience with literary convention.

Ironically, Clare's hypochondriacal tendency was provoked by the very conditions supposed to preclude it. As Lafford argues, Clare, the agricultural labourer, with his life of intense physical exertion, should have had no time for introspection and therefore 'should not have been susceptible to hypochondria', an affliction that was 'framed along class and occupational boundaries'.[34] However, these strenuous conditions contributed to the fluctuations between well and unwell, exacerbating the hypochondria which inflects his poetry. It was not just his imagination that catalysed somatic distress; there were physical and environmental provocations that made his melancholic poetic voice 'hypersensitive', specifically to itch.[35] In 'The Poets Wish', Clare depicts a struggling writer attempting to reconcile the creative demands of poetic inspiration with the domestic constraints of generating income and paying bills. The speaker confesses 'tis not for thoughts of being rich / That makes my wishing spirit itch', and instead modestly wishes to sit 'betwixt the little & the great', in 'a comfortable seat'.[36] Here, the speaker's 'itch' is not entirely provoked by a compulsion to rhyme, and emerges from a desire for adequate comfort and a respite from the demands of his agricultural lifestyle. At the poem's end, Clare's poet resigns himself to the fact that he must write poetry to pay his bills:

> He heavd a sigh and scratchd his head
> & Credits mouth wi' promise fed
> Then Set in terror down again
> Invok'd the muse and scrig'd a strain
> A trifling somthing glad to get
> To earn a dinner & discharge the debt (ll. 79-84)

By parallelling the verb phrase 'scratchd his head' with 'scrig'd a strain', Clare augments the aural association between 'scratchd' and 'scrig'd', consequently enjoining the mind, scratching hand, and poetic composition. Burton suggests writing as an antidote to melancholy, stating 'one must needs scratch where it itcheth',[37] and so the peasant figure is compelled to scratch to invoke 'the muse', forcing the internal itch that has previously arrived unbidden. In this case the itch that he must satisfy has a utilitarian genesis, and economics informs composition. The poet must 'scratch' or starve, and this is why the peasant figure in the poem sits 'in terror'. He must 'earn a dinner [to] discharge a debt', providing insight into the frequent material causes of the speaker's itch. His 'wishing spirit' might itch for a 'comfortable seat' to 'read & study' (l. 26), but the reality is that poetry is labour. The speaker's situation presciently demonstrates the frustrating and restless process of 'continuing physiological adjustment' that Rosenburg articulates. Clare's first biographer, Frederick Martin, records the opinion of Clare's doctor (visiting in 1823) that 'the illness of the poet was mainly the effect of poverty',[38] and Clare's peasant is acutely aware that without writing as a source of income, his body, deprived of money, while always being 'in a state of becoming', is left in 'jeopardy'. The conditions Clare depicts in 'The Poets Wish' might align with a literary trend for the materially distressed, melancholic poetic genius; however, the economic pressures of Clare's life were not fanciful, but substantial and tangible, and caused necessary adjustment to physiological irritation uniquely communicated through a vocabulary of itching manifested in a hypochondriacal disposition.

The itching body, in its unremarkable surroundings, 'Set in terror', is strikingly imbricated with the language of the sublime and Burkean terror. Considering the sublime in relation to Clare may seem counterintuitive, given his meticulous observation of nature's little, ordinary and often fugitive flora and fauna. Whilst Edward Strickland concedes that the sublime may be found in a few of the asylum poems, he also concludes that 'in general, Clare's equation of the simple and normal – the commonplace in fact – with the sublime runs counter to the whole tradition'. Strickland erroneously believes that Clare lacks the capacity for sublime expression or emotion and assumes no psychological depth beyond the 'jolly-ploughboy persona'. However, encountering 'terror' in the commonplace allows Clare to concentrate the grandeur of sublime expression into localised physiological irritation, connecting the sublime, the body, and composition to illuminate the manner in which his itching and fevered body shapes the creative process.[39]

Not only does the sublime inform a view of Clare as an itching and inflamed poet, but even Taylor repurposes the language of sublime obscurity in the introductory commentary on 'Dawning of Genius'. Although he may be aestheticising Clare's status as a peasant poet, Taylor proposes that 'there is, perhaps, no feeling so distressing as this to the individual: it is an irremovable nightmare as it were, to genius, which struggles in vain for sounds to convey an idea of its most intolerable sensations'; this is the poet 'Set in terror'.[40] The prospect of language failing after exhaustive efforts to write poetry terrifies Clare. At the end of 'Dawning of Genius', the speaker is tormented by dissatisfaction and inadequacy:

> Vain burns the soul & throbs the fluttering heart
> Their painfull pleasing feelings to impart
> Till by successless sallies wearied quite
> The memory fails & fancy takes her flight
> The wickett nipt within its socket dies
> Born down & smother'd in a thousand sighs[41]

Clare's anxieties about the failure of language recall Rosenburg's state of 'jeopardy', as the body 'burns', 'throbs', then 'fails' to settle into composed articulation. The spent candle, a synecdoche

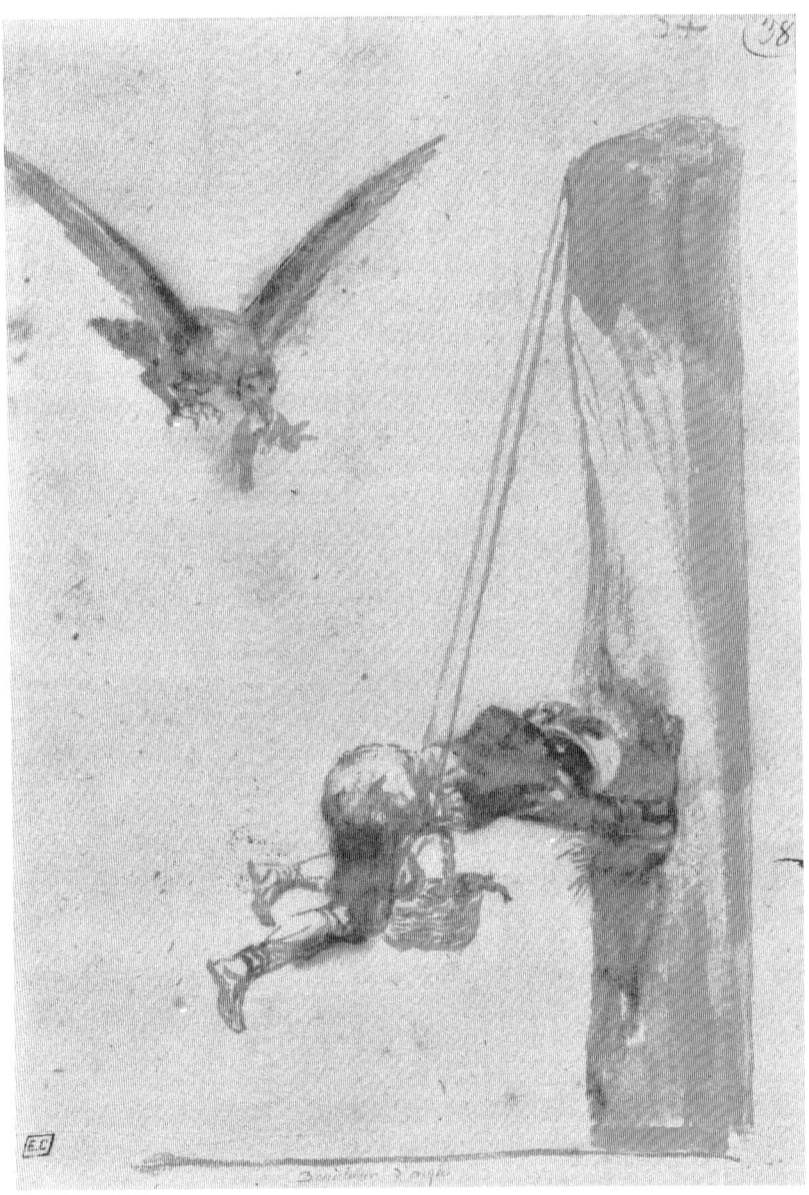

'The Eagle Hunter' (c. 1812–1820), Francisco José de Goya y Lucientes. The J. Paul Getty Museum, Los Angeles. Digital image courtesy of Getty's Open Content Program.

for genius, compresses the 'soul', 'heart', 'memory', and 'fancy' into a wick that gutters and then is 'smother'd in a thousand sighs', consequently exemplifying the debilitation of unfulfilled expression. Here, Clare evokes Edmund Burke's definition of the sublime as that which 'is fitted in any sort to excite the ideas of pain, and danger [...] or operates in a manner analogous to terror'.[42] 'Dawnings of Genius' depicts the creative process through sublime 'terror', but also explores how, as mentioned earlier, sublimity operates at 'the point at which language breaks down, yet where one feels that there is something to express or communicate'.[43] The association between sublimity, burning, and the itch of an incomplete articulation (oxymoronically qualified as 'painfull pleasing feeling[s]'), is evident earlier in the poem as the shepherd's 'inward powers inflame / & joys delight him which he cannot name' (ll. 25-6). Samuel Johnson defines 'inflame' as 'to set on fire; to make burn', additionally recognising its further meaning: 'to provoke; to irritate', which precisely intersects the heat vocabulary of the sublime with the specific medicalised language Clare chooses to communicate his aggravating, itching disposition.[44]

Running counter to this sublime 'terror' involved in the compositional process, is Clare's own conception of sublimity in literature. In a letter responding to Taylor's request for an essay on 'The Sublime and Beautiful in Poetry', Clare confidently refutes orthodox conceptions of sublimity, dismissing pretentious, grandiloquent examples as 'nothing more then a series of bomb bursting images taggd together by big sounding words to represent shadows or creations of the terrible but having no more effect on the mind as terrible then the unmeaning rant of a maniac'.[45] Clare conscientiously demonstrates how terror can be located in the simple and commonplace, and, unsurprisingly, he despises attempts to elevate natural phenomena through ostentatious metaphor or to 'mechanically yield the sublime' by heightening the unreal.[46] Indeed, in a subsequent letter to Taylor, Clare celebrates the sublime in Chaucer, whose 'descriptions of nature are so true to nature as to appear as fresh as if written yesterday'. Clare admires how 'his very simplicity is sublimity & his truth is the beautiful', demonstrating an awareness of the difference between encountering the sublime as 'terror' as a writer, and encountering the sublime as 'beautiful' as a reader.[47] As previously mentioned, when discussing 'An Effusion to Poetry', Clare views poetry as a 'cordial' to his constantly sensitised, itching body. Specifically though, he achieves momentary respite from the itch when he records sublimity from observations on a miniature scale with painstaking precision. The 'freshness' Clare admires in Chaucer's sublime is unexpectedly augmented by Jane Bennet's contemporary theory of enchantment. Bennet argues that 'to be enchanted is to be struck and shaken by the extraordinary that lives amid the familiar and the everyday'; to exist in a 'moment of pure presence'.[48] Situating Bennet's notion of enchantment within the context of an 'itch-scratch-itch' cycle reveals a paradox: while enchanting poetry acts as a 'cordial', a mental scratch for the itch, pursuing sublime expression in poetry engenders the itch in the first place. Clare articulates this frustration in a letter to Henry Cary: 'I hum & sing inwardly those little madrigals & then go in & pen them down [...] I look over them again & then the charm vanishes into the vanity that I shall do somthing better ere I die & so in spite of myself I ryhme on'.[49] While writing poetry may be terrifying, as it is in 'The Poet's Wish', Clare constantly pursues the 'charm' of sublime expression, even if that experience provides only a momentary relief from the restless activity of 'ryhm[ing] on'.

This sublime, restorative 'charm' is captured in poems that intensely fixate upon the miniature features of Clare's landscape. Poems that depict a sustained confrontation with miniscule detail not only accord with Clare's ideal sublime, but, 'in spite of' Clare's dissatisfaction, they achieve and retain the 'charm' that he believes is elusive. Clare constructs an enchanting moment of 'pure presence' in 'Clock A Clay'. Here Clare's unadorned expression reproduces the sublime simplicity and beauty he admires in Chaucer, but he also condenses two conflicting sublime experiences into the poem: the beautifully simple, and the terrifying. The microcosmic world of the tiny ladybird is hazardous and threatening: its 'gold home rocks as like to fall / On its pillars green and tall' and 'shakes in wind and showers'.[50] However the 'clock a clay' must endure this shocking peril. By amalgamating sublime grandeur, terror and beauty, with his own local observations and vernacular, Clare achieves sublimity in 'simplicity'. Clare realises a sublime experience more commonly associated with sweeping panoramas through a contraction of scale that compresses time and an implied architectural grandeur (a 'Pale green pillar'), into the microcosmic perspective of the ladybird. This distortion of scale is augmented as Clare associates the miniscule ladybird, so grounded in its natural habitat, with the abstract immensity of time. By punning on the association of the colloquial name for ladybird with a timepiece, Clare grants his beetle the eternal, omniscient responsibility of 'waiting' (l. 6) and 'watching' for the 'time of day'. Yet, this does not uncouple the ladybird from its familiar place underneath the flower; instead, Clare contracts the magnitude of time into a microcosmic corner of nature. At the end of 'Clock A Clay' the ladybird remains 'watching for the time of day'; the beetle exists, enchantingly, in 'pure presence' while constantly adjusting to the tempestuous elements. Its final, humble, yet remarkable assertion, 'here still I live lone clock a clay', mobilises 'still', a word that is freighted with ambiguity as part of a nexus of itching connotations, and which indicates restless endurance. The present continuous affirms 'still' as perpetuity, underscoring how the ladybird exists in time, and, therefore, inevitably in a state of jeopardy. If itching is a clear physiological indicator of a body 'in a state of becoming' and undergoing constant psychophysiological regeneration, then the sublime experience that Clare documents in this poem, characterised by endurance that involves continual adjustment to jeopardy, can be read as a state of itching. Precisely though, this state of jeopardy is vitalising. The quietly persistent ladybird, juxtaposed to the microcosmic but nonetheless sublime events, is sublime by the very fact of its simple endurance: eternally adjusting, and indeed itching, in time.

Intrinsic to the itch motif is the pain and pleasure that writing poetry causes Clare: with this itch to write comes adversity and suffering. Summarising Edward Drury's assessment of Clare, Bate notes that poetry was a 'kind of compulsion', trapping Clare into a 'potentially catastrophic circle of symptoms',[51] culminating in Northampton Lunatic Asylum, where the cause of his insanity was recorded as 'years addicted to poetical prosing'.[52] Whether this 'poetical prosing' is figured as an addiction, a compulsion, or a mania, inevitably it operated within a continuous cycle of aggravation and alleviation in which Clare both struggled and prospered. Importantly, though, that cycle is not only an affliction: there is relief. While the itch may have its distressing side, an itch anticipates an urge to scratch, and anticipation is in Clare's words 'the sweetest of earthly pleasures'.[53] Despite the perpetual restlessness of 'itching after ryhme', Clare was also hopeful, anticipating moments best defined as 'enchantments' in which poetry offered relief. Even though a causal link is associated between this compulsion to write and his eventual decline, Clare recognised that discomfort was integral to producing poetry. Consequently, the 'itch-scratch-itch' cycle provides a new hermeneutic by which

Clare's compositional process can be examined. In one letter to Taylor, he regretted 'writing smoothly with little sense';[54] this smooth, senseless writing was not typical of Clare who creatively benefited from, to borrow from Rosenburg, 'jeopardy'. Clare confesses: 'I wrote because it pleased me – in sorrow & when I am happy it makes me happier'.[55] Poetry was not a restful luxury for Clare, it was a difficult but often gratifying exertion, a state best expressed in 'The Harvest Morning' in which the landscape itches with lively and tireless 'busy bustling toil', and where the arduous tasks of the farmer continually renew.[56] Clare's pruriceptive style, informed by the restlessly itching, adjusting, indeed 'becoming' body, communicates at once the anxiety writing caused him, his constant efforts to make sense of the psychophysiological turmoil of composition, and the 'enchantment' he found in producing poetry.

NOTES

1. *By Himself*, p. 17.
2. James Mckusick, describing Clare's poems as written in the 'vernacular discourse of stubborn locality', considers Clare's efforts to educate himself alongside his unique linguistic experimentation in 'John Clare and the Tyranny of Grammar', *Studies in Romanticism*, 33.2 (1994), 255–77 (p. 263; p. 274).
3. Itch, or pruritus, is defined in modern medical science as 'an unpleasant sensation that leads to the need to scratch [...] to achieve the "pleasure" derived from scratching' by Laurent Misery and Sabine Dutray, 'Psychogenic Itch', *Translational Psychiatry*, 8.52 (2018), 1-8 (p. 1; p. 5).
4. 'To An Infant Daughter', *Early Poems*, II, pp. 391-2, l. 24; l. 31. Hereafter, all references to poems taken from these editions appear after the first quotation.
5. 'The Progress of Ryhme', *Middle Period*, III, pp. 492-503, l. 204.
6. Charles Rosenburg, 'The Therapeutic Revolution: Medicine, Meaning and Social Change in Nineteenth Century America', *Perspectives in Biology and Medicine*, 20.4 (1977), 489-506 (p. 487).
7. Misery and Dutray, 'Psychogenic Itch', p. 5.
8. See C. Potenzieri and B. J. Undem, 'Basic Mechanisms of Itch', *Clinical and Experimental Allergy*, 42 (2011), 8-19 (p. 8), for a comprehensive aetiology of itching.
9. John Clare, Letter to James Augustus Hessey, 2 April 1822, *Letters*, pp. 235-6 (p. 235).
10. 'Prurience', Samuel Johnson, *A Dictionary of the English Language*, 4th edn, 2 vols (London: W. Strahan *et al*, 1773), II [no pagination].
11. *By Himself*, p. 7; p. 77-8.
12. Letter to John Taylor, 21 December 1820, *Letters*, pp. 123-5 (p. 124).
13. Letter to John Taylor, 14 June 1821, *Letters*, pp. 196-8 (p. 198).
14. Letter to John Taylor, 18 December 1821, *Letters*, pp. 219-22 (p. 221).
15. Rosenburg, 'The Therapeutic Revolution', p. 487.

16. Michael Nicholson, 'Common Distress: John Clare's Poetic Strain', in *Palgrave Advances in John Clare Studies*, ed. by Simon Kövesi and Erin Lafford (London: Palgrave Macmillan, 2020), pp. 221-41 (p. 223; p. 227; p. 239).
17. Misery and Dutray, 'Psychogenic Itch', p. 5.
18. Murray Krieger, *Ekphrasis: The Illusion of the Natural Sign* (Baltimore; London: Johns Hopkins University Press, 2019), p. 268.
19. Rosenburg, 'The Therapeutic Revolution', p. 487.
20. Sarah Houghton-Walker, 'Enkindling Ecstasy: The Sublime Vision of John Clare', *Romanticism*, 9.2 (2008), 176-95 (p. 185).
21. R. Paus, M. Schmelz, T. Biro, and M. Steinhoff, 'Frontiers in Pruritus Research: Scratching the Brain for More Effective Itch Therapy', *Journal of Clinical Investigation*, 116.5 (2006), 1174-86 (p. 1174).
22. John Taylor, 'Introduction' to John Clare, *Poems Descriptive of Rural Life and Scenery* (London: Taylor and Hessey, 1820), pp. vii-xxviii (p. vii).
23. George Rousseau, 'Coleridge's Dreaming Gut: Digestion, Genius, Hypochondria', in *Cultures of the Abdomen: Diet, Digestion, and Fat in the Modern World*, ed. by Christopher Forth and Ana Carden-Coyne (Basingstoke: Palgrave Macmillan, 2005), pp. 105-26 (p. 109).
24. *By Himself*, p. 29.
25. *Biography*, p. 410.
26. Robert Burton, *The Anatomy of Melancholy*, ed. by T. C. Faulkner, N. K. Kiessling and R. L. Blair, 6 vols (1621; Oxford: Clarendon Press, 1989), I, p. 119; p. 429.
27. Misery and Dutray, 'Psychogenic Itch', p. 2.
28. Heather R. Beatty, *Nervous Disease in Late Eighteenth-Century Britian* (London: Pickering and Chatto, 2012), p. 9.
29. Erin Lafford, '"Fancys or Feelings": John Clare's Hypochondriac Poetics', in *Palgrave Advances in John Clare Studies*, ed. by Simon Kövesi and Erin Lafford (London: Palgrave Macmillan, 2020), pp. 249-73 (p. 259; p. 251; p. 255).
30. Letter to John Taylor, 7 March 1831, *Letters*, pp. 536-8 (p. 537).
31. M.D. Avia and M.A. Ruiz, 'Recommendations for the Treatment of Hypochondriac Patients', *Journal of Contemporary Psychotherapy*, 35.3 (2005), 301-13 (p. 301).
32. 'An Effusion to Poesy', *Early Poems*, I, pp. 545-6, ll. 19-22.
33. Rousseau, 'Coleridge's Dreaming Gut: Digestion, Genius, Hypochondria', p. 108.
34. Lafford, '"Fancys or Feelings": John Clare's Hypochondriac Poetics', p. 255.
35. Rousseau, 'Coleridge's Dreaming Gut: Digestion, Genius, Hypochondria', p. 108.
36. 'The Poets Wish', *Early Poems*, I, pp. 489-92, ll. 17-8; l. 20; l. 23.
37. Burton, *The Anatomy of Melancholy*, I, p. 7.
38. Fredrick Martin, *The Life of John Clare* (London and Cambridge: Macmillan, 1865), p. 173.
39. Edward Strickland, 'John Clare and the Sublime', *Criticism*, 29.2 (1987), 141-161 (p. 154 and 156).
40. John Taylor, 'Introduction' to *Poems Descriptive*, p. xiii.
41. 'Dawning of Genius', *Early Poems*, I, pp. 451-2, ll. 47-52.
42. Edmund Burke, *A Philosophical Enquiry into the Origin of our Ideas of Sublime and Beautiful*, ed. by Paul Guyer (Oxford: Oxford University Press, 2015), p. 33.

43   Houghton-Walker, 'Enkindling Ecstasy: The Sublime Vision of John Clare', p. 185.
44   'Inflame', Samuel Johnson, *A Dictionary of the English Language*.
45   Letter to John Taylor, 15 April 1831, *Letters*, p. 539.
46   Ross Wilson, 'Clare and The Sublime', in *The Cambridge Companion to John Clare*, ed. by Sarah Houghton-Walker (Cambridge University Press, 2024), pp. 60-73 (p. 62).
47   Letter to John Taylor, May? 1831, *Letters*, p. 540.
48   Jane Bennet, *The Enchantments of Modern Life: Attachments, Crossings, Ethics* (Princeton University Press, 2001), p. 4.
49   Letter to Henry Francis Cary, after 20 October 1832, *Letters*, pp. 594-6 (pp. 595-6).
50   'Clock A Clay', *Later Poems*, I, pp. 611-12, ll. 19-24.
51   *Biography*, p. 147.
52   John Clare Collection in Peterborough Central Library, Manuscript F4: 'Certificate of application for the admission of John Clare, No. 354, to Northampton General Lunatic Asylum, dated 28th December, 1814'. I am grateful to Elisabeth Kingston and Gail Richardson for assistance in consulting these manuscripts. Peterborough Manuscript references follow Margaret Grainger's *A Descriptive Catalogue of the John Clare Collection in Peterborough Museum and Art Gallery* (Peterborough: printed for Earl Fitzwilliam, 1973).
53   *By Himself*, p. 57.
54   Letter to John Taylor, 2 January 1821, *Letters*, pp. 130-2 (p. 131).
55   Letter to Thomas Pringle, 8 February 1832, *Letters*, pp. 571-3 (p. 572).
56   'The Harvest Morning', *Early Poems*, I, pp. 434-6, l. 9.

I Am! Again
Mark Fiddes

"I long for scenes where man hath never trod,"
   John Clare

We pick between rocks on the wadi floor
as Jabal Jais rises in stone ghazals.
John Clare remarks on the land's masonry,
its architraves, stairways and balustrades,
as if a grand house had been excavated
from cliffs leaving only a cracked facia
with scorpions and darkling beetles seamed
into curtains and dusty tapestries.
He plucks a primula for his lapel.
By a flame-speared dragon tree, he explains
why bee-eaters sing the love songs of scree,
that every silence is a life God breathes
into the domains we have forsaken.
It is a long hike back to the madhouse.
We reach the emerald pools left by floods.
"And the fish?" I ask, unlacing my boots.
"Invisible, but you can still feel them."
He dangles his feet which are hairier
than I believed, his horny toes cloven.
His coat's become a sandy, matted fleece.
He lifts his amber gaze above to bleat:
"If Jacob can scale an angel's ladder,
then why, in all that's heavenly, can't we?"

Help John Clare escape Epping and guide his journey home

'A must play for anyone interested in interactive storytelling, education and video games'

GameMaker

www.claresescape.com

'And soon the wisper went about the town': Gossips and gossiping in John Clare's narrative poetry

Emlyn David

A collective conception of stories and meaning

Gossips are everywhere in Clare's poetry. They are members of the community that is represented in Clare's poems, and they often occupy a key function in his texts. They sometimes are the narrators of tales told within a frame narrative, and their recurring presence in the background of some poems underlines their cultural importance. They are the keepers of stories and customs in the community and they pass down knowledge to younger generations. Their tales function as cautionary tales, but they are also presented as skilled storytellers. Clare presents gossips as influential figures in his development as a poet. Listening to 'gossips' stories' enables Lubin to become a storyteller himself in 'The Village Minstrel' (1821). The fact that their voices resonate throughout Clare's poetry is once again proof that the voices of non-elite people are valued in his poems.

Exploring the role of gossips in Clare's poems is at the intersection of a current interest in Romantic auralities, so vitally important when looking at Clare's works, and already existing criticism on Clare's narrative art, more specifically on the narrators of Clare's poems. According to Mina Gorji, the emphasis Clare places on listening is a defining characteristic of his poetic voice: 'Clare's sensitivity as a listener includes a responsiveness to the listening of others, of birds, animals, other poets, and even of the landscape itself'.[1] The concept of 'lyric ear', developed by Claire Marie Stancek offers interesting insights on the question of Romantic listening.[2] It explores a different aspect of Romantic poetry, in a field that has often focused on the importance of sight or voice in the works of Romantic authors.

Listening is more than a motif in Clare's poetry – it is a founding principle of his poetics.

Several works have focused on Clare's attentiveness to the sounds that can be heard in nature, underlining his capacity to transcribe birdsong in his poems.[3] Scenes of storytelling also reveal how central the concept of listening is in Clare's works. These scenes raise questions concerning the representation of multiple marginal voices and about the linguistic tools used to represent such diversity – for example the use of dialect. The representation of voices and listening in the text has a textual, political and ethical dimension.[4]

Gossips are often storytellers in Clare's poems. John Goodridge dedicated several articles and chapters to the craft of female narrators in Clare's texts.[5] These storytellers have a vital function in the community, being 'the guardians of narrative and folkloric wisdom, the unofficial educators and archivists of rural popular culture'.[6] Goodridge points to the echoes that can be found between the narrators' techniques and the poet's own narrative strategies in the introductions to his embedded tales. Building upon this, this article explores the place and role of gossips and gossiping in a selection of Clare's narrative poems. It argues that gossips become an emblem for a specific type of discourse and a specific poetic practice. Gossiping is envisioned as a collective meaning making process, and gossips and gossiping are celebrated as a worthy source of inspiration by Clare.

The different meanings of the term 'gossip' link it to the question of community. According to the *Oxford English Dictionary*, the noun 'gossip' originally refers to a godparent: 'one who has contracted spiritual affinity with another by acting as a sponsor at a baptism' (*OED* 1). The entry 'gossips' in Baker's *Glossary* gives a similar definition: 'sponsors at a christening'.[7] Both sources indicate that the term evolved from 'god-sib': 'the Anglo-Saxon word for god-father or god-mother; signifying a spiritual relationship to each other, and to the child for which they are responsible in baptism, through the performance of a religious rite or ceremony'.[8] The word is associated with the creation of strong spiritual and social connections in a community.

The second definition of the term refers to a friend: 'a familiar acquaintance, friend, chum. Formerly applied to both sexes, now only (somewhat archaic) to women' (first recorded use 1390, *OED* 2). Definition 2b makes specific reference to a group of female friends invited to be present at a birth (first recorded use 1600). The first two meanings of the verb 'to gossip' are linked with these definitions. To gossip originally means 'to be a gossip or sponsor to' (*OED* 1) or 'to act as a gossip, or familiar acquaintance; to take part (in a feast), to be a boon-companion; to make oneself at home' (*OED* 2), thus taking up the connotations that associate gossips with spiritual guardians or familiar figures. These definitions suggest that gossips were considered to be central figures in a community, being advisory figures associated with moral responsibility.

The third meaning of term is familiar to modern-day readers: 'a person, mostly a woman, of light and trifling character, especially one who delights in idle talk; a newsmonger, a tattler' (first recorded use 1566, *OED* 3). The fourth definition of the term extends this to refer to a type of conversation characteristic of gossips: 'the conversation of such person; idle talk; trifling or groundless rumour; tittle-tattle. Also, in a more favourable sense: easy, unrestrained talk or writing, especially about persons or social incidents' (first recorded use 1811, *OED* 4). The third definition of the verb extends from the noun: 'to talk idly, mostly about people's affairs, to go about tattling' (first recorded use 1627, *OED* 3a). By the time Clare was writing, a 'gossip' could refer to these four definitions. This article aims to examine how Clare's poems incorporate elements from these different definitions to bring forth the cultural importance of gossips.

Several of the narrators in Clare's poems correspond to these definitions. The narrator in 'Valentine Eve' is referred to as a gossip: '"Aye" said a gossip by a neighbours hearth' (l. 9).[9] The name 'Goody', used for the narrator of 'The Two Soldiers' and of 'The Cross Roads' is a reference to an old woman, often a widow, and can be associated with this type of character. The narrator in 'The Sorrows of Love' (composed between February 1822 and November 1824) also evokes a woman who fits such description. The villagers suspect her of being a witch:

> "Here the old woman for wants small rewards
> "Woud tell our fortunes both by cups & cards
> "Some calld her witch & wisperd all they dare
> "Of nightly things that had been noticd there
> "Witches of every shape that usd to meet
> "To count the stars or mutterd charms repeat (ll. 175-80)[10]

The description of the 'droll old woman' is reminiscent of 'the woman of trifling character' (*OED* meaning 3), but the narrator depicts her in a more positive light, insisting on her playful character:

"Yet she to us appeard like other folks
"A droll old woman full of tales & jokes (ll. 193-4)[11]

In 'The Cross Roads', Goody is surrounded with old women who tell one another anecdotes: 'The song & tale an hours restraint relieves / & while the old dames gossip at their ease.' (l. 8-9), thus bringing to mind the image of a community of female friends evoked by *OED* meaning 2.[12] A similar character tells Richard about an old custom in 'The Rivals: A Pastoral': 'An old droll woman who first told it me / Vowd that a truer token coud not be' (l. 39-40).[13] Gossips are represented as motors in the circulation of stories and customs.

They are the keepers of the stories of older generations and local customs. They are associated with a type of knowledge transmission that ensures a form of continuity among a community. Gossiping, however, concerns a form of fragmentary knowledge, one that is partial and transformed as it is transmitted. The verb refers to a particular mode of spreading information. These connotations can be found in the metaphorical use of the term in 'January: A Winter's Day':

> Now, musing o'er the changing scene,
> Farmers behind the tavern-screen
> Collect; – with elbow idly press'd
> On hob, reclines the corner's guest,
> Reading the news, to mark again
> The bankrupt lists, or price of grain;
> Or old Moore's annual prophecies
> Of flooded fields and clouded skies;
> Whose Almanac's thumb'd pages swarm
> With frost and snow, and many a storm,
> And wisdom, gossip'd from the stars,
> Of politics and bloody wars. (ll. 7-18)[14]

These lines are quoted in the *OED* as an example of the fourth definition of the verb: 'To tell like a gossip, to communicate' (first recorded use 1611, *OED* 4). They evoke the fragmentary and collaborative dimension of the type of knowledge that is shared through the composite nature of almanacs and the image of the stars in the sky. The term has no derogatory connotations, since reading signs in the sky leads to the acquisition of 'wisdom' (l. 17).

Gossips and gossiping conjure up the idea of a collective type of discourse, and the ways it spreads. Clare provides an example of this

'They are Dying' (c. 1825–1828), Francisco José de Goya y Lucientes. The J. Paul Getty Museum, Los Angeles. Digital image courtesy of Getty's Open Content Program.

in 'Valentine Eve', which was composed in 1824 but never published in his lifetime. When a mysterious stranger arrives in the village, the inhabitants make conjectures about his identity (the fifth line of this quotation is followed by an indication of its metrical pattern, following Derek Attridge's model[15]):

> & many a guess from rumours whispers fell
> & gossips daily had new tales to tell
> Some said he once had been a wealthy man
> & from a bankrupts painful ruin ran
> Others with far worse causes marked his flight
> O   b   o   B   O   B o   B   o   B
> & taxed him with a forgers name out right
> & tho he heard such whispers passing bye
> Hed laugh but never stop to question why (ll. 45-52)[16]

These lines stage the way in which events are caught up in a network of speech. The promoted offbeat 'worse' highlights the implicit dimension of what is said. The rhythmic nucleus formed by the periphrasis 'far worst causes' evokes the act of gossiping, which hinges on allusion and understatement. These forms of speech constitute filters that sway the characters' interpretation of the events. These rumours are foregrounded by Clare even though they develop on the side of the narrative. The passage underlines the speculative dimension of this process. The mere 'rumours' and 'whispers' (l. 45) turn into structured narratives – 'tales' (l. 46) – the number of which keeps increasing.

If gossiping is a striking representation of a collaborative and self-generative type of speech, some of Clare's poems underscore its potentially destructive dimension. In 'The Cross Roads', written in 1829 and first published in *The Village Minstrel*, Goody insists on how fast rumours about her friend Jane spread:

> "& soon the wisper went about the town
> "That Janes good looks procurd her many a gown
> "From him whose promise was to every one
> "But whose intention was to wive with none
> "Twas nought to wonder tho begun by guess
> "For Jane was lovly in her sunday dress
> "& all expected such a rosey face
> "Woud be her ruin – as was just the case
> "The while the change was easily percievd
> "Some months went by ere I such tales believd (ll. 65-74)[17]

The way in which stories and rumours spread in this passage is quite similar to what can be observed in 'Valentine Eve', but the tone is significantly darker. The sounds of the passage move from [s], [w] and [t] (l. 65) through 'the wisper' – which establishes a connection between 'soon' and 'went' – and 'went' – which connects the [w] sound at the beginning of the line and the alliteration [t] at the end of the line. The chain of sounds established here can thus evoke the way in which rumours about Jane are spread among the town and are transformed as they are repeated.

The periphrasis 'him whose promise was to every one' can be read as free indirect speech, as the phrase creates the illusion to take up the terms used by the inhabitants themselves. These lines can be read as a representation of how the narrative is contaminated by gossip. The destructive dimension of slander is foregrounded (ll. 89 and 90), and Jane's detractors are designated as 'enemies' who distort reality through a type of speech that appear almost self-fulfilling: 'Tho foes made double what they heard of all / Swore lies as proofs and prophysied her fall'. When Goody mentions that stories are still told about Jane after her death, she denounces the cruelty of such behaviour while highlighting the long-lasting influence of such tales:

"For every tongue was loosd to gabble oer
"The slanderous things that secrets passd before
"Wi truth or lies they neednt then be strickt
"The one they raild at coudnt contradict (ll. 157-60)[18]

Just like the narrator in 'Valentine Eve', Goody choses to tell a story that matches the place and moment of the telling, stories that will work as cautionary tales for the young women in their audience. The educative purpose of these stories brings back the godparent role of the original word. The gossip is not the one who engages in 'idle talk' here, but rather the one who warns young women against the mistakes they might make and the ways in which their community react to such mistakes. These poems make explicit the links between gossips and moral guidance, since the stories told by these narrators synthetise the values of a community. As she tells the story to a group of young women, Goody takes part in the survival of the narrative, providing herself an illustration of the fact that Jane's story outlives her friend, whether it be through the stories told by the villagers or the moments of storytelling, like the one presented in the poem.

According to Stancek, the motif of the gossip is a privileged metaphor for the relationship between narrator and reader: 'Gossip functions as a metaphor for the intimate relationship between a narrator and a reader, as well as for the voyeuristic gaze of a narrator watching characters'.[19] This correspondence reinforces the metaliterary dimension of Clare's poems, by turning the reader into one of the members of the audience of his narrators, or of the poetic voice. The motif of the gossip becomes an emblem for a specific type of discourse, a specific conception of narrative art and of poetic practice. Clare does not associate gossip with a loss of meaning, but rather presents it as a multiple and collaborative meaning-making process.

Feminine traditions of storytelling and the Romantic poet

The fact that Clare gives pride of place to gossips in his poetry reasserts the cultural importance of an often frowned-upon figure. Clare's poems foreground how gossiping creates links within a community. They illustrate the idea that gossips promote a form of cohesion within a neighbourhood or a village, as Capp notes: '[...] gossiping was about bonding and belonging'.[20] Sharing anecdotes, information and stories strengthens the links between the gossips, but gossips are also the moral protectors of a larger community: '[The informal networks to which women turned for help in personal disputes] could be used to force recalcitrant neighbours to conform to locally accepted codes of behaviour, or to protect the interests and reputation of the parish as a whole'.[21] The evocation of gossiping and popular traditions such as storytelling must therefore be reinscribed within the historical development of a gendered conception of speech.

The tales shared by gossips, but also the popular traditions represented in Clare's poems, have been historically associated with a feminine mode of discourse. This type of speech is often discredited:

> Adam Fox identifies a misogynous backlash against women's speech, sociable dialogue and forms of oral narrative, which he identifies with the 'rhetoric of the Reformation' and the rise of rationalistic and scientific discourse.[22]

As a character type, the gossip stands at the intersection of misogynistic associations between elderly women and devalued forms of speech. This can be observed in *OED* meaning 3, which insists on the 'idle and trifling character' of gossips. Modes of conversation associated with gossips are considered to be marginal. Even if the poetic project of the Romantics was to integrate the language of conversation into their poetry, gossips represent a type of conversation that does not correspond to the poetic codes of the time: 'Minimized, feminized, and shunned, gossip stands 'by the side of' traditional gentlemanly forms of conversation'.[23] The recurring representation of gossips and gossiping enables Clare to rehabilitate this figure by acknowledging the influence of these modes of discourse on his poetry.

The gossips represented in Clare's poems constitute a major alternative to the conventional image of the Romantic poet – a young male poet whose prophetic gifts enable him to spread his revelations through his words. Although the poet's originality comes from his ability to extract and express universal truths from his personal experience, the poet is often presented as the omnipotent origin of the poetic voice. He is the only origin of the text and transcribes his ability to be in communion with the world. On the contrary, the emphasis that Clare places on repetition and stories passed down generations constitutes according to Fiona Stafford, 'a quiet challenge to the prevailing emphasis on originality or novelty'.[24] Clare develops a poetic practice that focuses on the multiple versions of stories and the multiplicity of voices rather than on the origin of his material.

The multiple versions given of the same story, and the multiple points of view presented in the poems often make it impossible to establish a definitive version of the events recounted. This can be observed in 'The Lodge House', written at the end of 1819. The day after the arrival of a mysterious stranger in the house, Hodge goes to the nearest village in order to shed light on the mystery of the previous night. The stories about the incident have spread across the town, but the young man learns nothing new: 'Hodge went to the village conjectures he heard / But nothing for truth never came' (ll. 263-4).[25] Sharing the story of the event is a collective reaction to the intrusion of a potential danger for the community. However, the stories shared in the village have a limited function. They do not enable Hodge to access any form of truth, since he is only confronted with every one's 'opinions' (l. 265).

The circulation of stories is thus sometimes associated with a loss of meaning, as the villagers are not represented as a reliable source of information. The subtitle of the poem, 'A Gossips Tale', indicates that it is impossible to identify the origin of the story that is told. The use of the indefinite article in the subtitle shows that it is not the precise origin of the narrative that is important, but rather the type of discursive tradition in which the poem can be reinscribed. The subtitle thus also functions as a marker that formally reinscribes the poem in a narrative tradition. Clare stages stories the origin of which has been lost. Their prime characteristics is to have been composed, transmitted and transformed collectively.

The discursive practices associated with gossips inspire the form of Clare's poems. The multiplication of points of view, the staging of circulating stories in a single poem, the explicit reference to a popular tradition of storytelling and the existence of multiple versions of the poems reveal a participatory conception of poetry. Clare celebrates the transformation of a material the origin of which cannot be identified, and which has already been appropriated. The importance of listening in his poetry comes from the importance of gossips, and the modes of discourse associated with them. The influence of this feminine tradition of storytelling is central, since Clare develops his poetic persona as one that is receptive to these marginal voices.

Clare and the concept of 'lyric ear'

Clare's poetic persona illustrates the idea that his poetic voice is a listener. Many of Clare's poems involve a description of moments of listening. Clare's poetry can thus be linked to Stancek's concept of 'the lyric ear' or 'speaking ear': 'the speaking ear involves a description of listening, which goes so far in its intensity or detail that it explicitly or implicitly figures the poem itself as an ear'.[26] Clare constantly invites his readers to listen to what surrounds them by adopting 'a pose of listening attention' himself.[27] Such a conception of poetry and writing pervades 'The Village Minstrel'.

The poem offers a reflection on the calling of a young poet and sketches a portrait of the poet that is in tune with Clare's aesthetics. Multiple passages in the poem present descriptions of scenes of storytelling. Strong emphasis is placed on the influence of such moments on Lubin's imagination:

> 13
> How ancient dames a faries anger feard
> From gossips stories lubin often heard
> How they but every night the hearthstone cleard
> & gen their visits all things neat prepard
> As fays nought more then cleanliness regard
> When in the morn they never faild to share
> Or gold or silver as their meet reward
> Dropt in the water superstitions care
> To make the charm succeed had cautious placed there

'The Gossips' (undated), Samuel Scott (1702-72),
Yale Center for British Art, Paul Mellon Collection.

> 14
> & thousands such the village keeps alive
> Beings that people superstitious earth
> That ere in rural manners will survive
> So long as wild rusticity has birth
> To spread their wonders round the cottage hearth
> On lubins mind oft deeply they imprest
> Oft fear forbid to share his neighbours mirth
> & long each tale by fancy newly drest
> Brought faireys in his dreams & broke his infant rest (ll. 109-26)[28]

The rhyme pairs 'feard' / 'cleard' and 'regard' / 'reward' highlight the educative dimension of the tale, which again conjures up the role of gossips as advisory figures. The story invites every listener to keep their home clean in order to avoid upsetting the fairies. Lubin adopts the 'pose of listening attention' evoked by Stancek, and the scene is one of the moments of 'joyful listening' (l. 77) evoked in the poem. Gossips are the ones who pass down local folklore, as the tales are referred to as 'gossips stories' (l. 110). The enchanting power of such tales is underlined. The stories are associated with the presence of benevolent supernatural beings. The 'wonders' spread 'round the cottage hearth' (l. 122) can be read as a reference to fairies and also to the stories told by the fireside.

These stories feed Lubin's imagination. Clare uses the word 'fancy' here (l. 125), which refers to the ability to combine and rearrange memories and perceptions and is one of the central concepts of Romantic theory.[29] The stories told by gossips impress Lubin deeply, and it is not surprising to find the term 'fancy' again in the following stanzas (ll. 131 and 135):

> Dread monsters fancy moulded on his sight
> Soft would he step lest they his tread shoud hear
> & crept & crept till past his wild afright
> Then on winds wings would rally as it where
> So swift the wild retreat of childhoods fancyd fear
>
> 16
> & when fear left him on his corner seat
> Much woud he chatter oer each dreadful tale
> Tell how he heard the sound of 'proaching feet
> & warriors gingling in their coats of mail (ll. 131-9)

'Peasant Woman and Dog on the Edge of a Forest', by follower of Pieter Pietersz (1749-1842). Harvard Art Museums/Fogg Museum, Gift of Belinda L. Randall from the collection of John Witt Randall.

Imagination is an organising force, since it shapes monsters before Lubin's eyes ('moulded' l. 131). This passage is preceded by the stanzas describing Lubin listening to gossips by the fireside. By telling the story of his adventures after the events, Lubin makes that experience his own, turning it into a tale in which the multiple frightening elements only further emphasize his fearlessness. This story signals Lubin's birth as a storyteller. The 'dreadful tales' (l. 137) are now the ones he tells, and no longer the ones others tell him. This movement reveals that Lubin's narrative practice directly stems from the tales he has heard during his childhood.

The customs evoked in these stanzas are presented as living traditions: '& thousands such the village keeps alive' (l. 118). The role of rural customs and the ones who pass them down, like gossips, is to keep this cultural heritage alive, as the rhyme 'alive' / 'survive' underlines (l. 108-10). If many Romantic authors share an interest in popular narrative and poetic forms, Clare represents them in a unique way. A comparison between passages taken from 'The Village Minstrel' and Wordsworth's 'The Solitary Reaper' reveals significant differences between distinct modes of Romantic listening. 'The Solitary Reaper' was written in 1805 and first published in *Poems, in Two Volumes* (1807). It shares similarities with 'The Village Minstrel': the two poems offer lively descriptions of a rural setting; they stem from their authors' interest in popular culture and they are based on the representation of the poet as a listener. In spite of such similarities, Wordsworth's poem insists on the distance between the poetic persona and the reaper. 'The Solitary Reaper' underlines the reaper's isolation through phrases like 'single in the field' (l. 1), 'singing by herself' (l. 3), and 'Alone she cuts' (l. 5). The relationship between the poet and the reaper is characterised by a sense of distance. The poet is a traveller and nothing more. He hears the song only briefly and there is no contact between the reaper and him.

The young reaper is thus a ghostly figure, an association that is further reinforced by the traditional personification of death as a reaper. Such an image invites readers to read the poem as the metaphorical representation of the disappearance of oral tradition, which becomes rare and confined to isolated regions. The uncertain fate of this song which may never be sung again, emerges: 'Some natural sorrow, loss, or pain / That has been, and may be again!' (ll. 23-4). Fiona Stafford notes that the importance of the notion of distance in that poem also constitutes a metaliterary comment on the poem: 'the medium is that of the printed word, with the distance between the words on the page and the living voice being acknowledged throughout'.[30] The reaper's song is indeed not represented in the poem:

> Will no one tell me what she sings?
> Perhaps the plaintive numbers flow
> For old, unhappy, far-off things,
> And battles long ago:
> Or is it some more humble lay,
> Familiar matter of today?
> Some natural sorrow, loss, or pain,
> That has been, and may be again! (ll. 17-24)[31]

According to Stafford, this song is one of the examples of the 'unheard melodies' in British Romanticism, as evoked by Keats in the 'Ode on a Grecian Urn'.[32] It is impossible to identify the topic of the song, its date and its origin. The reaper's song remains enigmatic because the real topic of the poem is the reception of the song by the poet rather than the song itself. The reflection offered on the idea of listening and the musicality of the poem is focused on the poet much more than on the voice to which he is listening: 'The poem celebrates the capacity of the mind to conjure up beautiful sounds from within'.[33] The reaper's voice only exists as far as it is perceived by the poet and conjured up by him.

The poet's mode of listening is intrinsically linked to his relation to the world. The poet's ability to represent the world is thus deeply political:

> By considering how lyric constructs the ear, rather than the voice, we can expand participation to include bodies, objects, and surroundings that share physical space, rather than simply those who have the agency or the privilege to speak.[34]

The different ways in which Clare and Wordsworth represent moments of listening in these poems reveals the existence of two different modes of lyric listening in their poetry. Wordsworth uses moments of listening as a way to develop a reflection on how the song resonates and lives in the poet's mind. He turns his poem into a commentary on the influence of traditional forms on his poetry, but also on their future. In 'The Village Minstrel', Clare foregrounds moments of exchange, and places emphasis on the representation of a community. Clare's poems constantly celebrate the voices that enable him to develop his own, whether it be older or contemporary poets, popular culture and the songs and stories from Helpston, or the voices of all the men and women associated with these forms of culture.

Even though it is still the voice of a single individual, Clare's voice is one made out of many. It is a perfect illustration of the conception of poetic voice developed by Susan Stewart: 'In listening, I am listening to the material history of your connection to all the dead and the living who have been impressed upon you. [...] The individual voice is in these ways demonic, mediating, traversing'.[35] Just like the gossips he celebrates in his poems, whose words spread in unpredictable ways, the poet is the mediator of words that are shared horizontally rather than vertically. He is not the repository of a transcendent type of knowledge but the one who spreads these numerous voices through his poetry. Clare's poetry represents different poetic and cultural traditions, and the multiple voices that keep these traditions alive. His poems invite readers to hear a multiplicity of marginal voices that are usually scorned and celebrate them as a valuable source of inspiration.

NOTES

1 Mina Gorji, 'John Clare and the Language of Listening', *Romanticism*, 26.2 (2020), 153-67 (155).

2 Claire Marie Stancek, 'Lyric Ear: Romantic Poetics of Listening' (unpublished doctoral thesis, UC Berkeley, 2018).

3 See for instance Stephanie Kuduk Weiner, 'Listening with John Clare', *Studies in Romanticism*, 48.3 (2009), 371-90 and Matthew Rowney, 'Music in the Noise: The Acoustic Ecology of John Clare', *Journal of Interdisciplinary Voice Studies*, 1.1 (2016), 23-40.

4 Stephanie Kuduk Weiner addresses the question of orality in 'John Clare's Speaking Voices: Dialect, Orality, and the Intermedial Poetic Text', *Essays in Romanticism*, 5.1 (2018), 85-100; for an interesting study of the influence of Clare's poems on the Northamptonshire dialect itself, see Alexander Broadhead, 'John Clare and the Northamptonshire Dialect: Rethinking Language and Place', *JCSJ*, 40 (2021), 47-68.

5 See John Goodridge, 'Telling Stories: Clare, Folk Culture, and Narrative Techniques', *Wordsworth Circle*, 29.3 (1998), 164-7 and his chapter 'Storytellings: "Old Women's Memorys"' in *John Clare and Community* (Cambridge University Press, 2013), pp. 169-89.

6 Goodridge, 'Telling Stories', p. 165.

7   Anne Elizabeth Baker, *Glossary of Northamptonshire Words and Phrases, with Examples of their Colloquial Use, and Illustrations from Various Authors: to which are added, the Customs of the County*, 2 vols (London: John Russell Smith, and Northampton: Abel & Sons, and Mark Dorman, 1854), I, p. 286.
8   Baker, *Glossary of Northamptonshire Words and Phrases*, p. 281.
9   *Cottage Tales*, p. 72.
10 *Cottage Tales*, pp. 86-7.
11 *Cottage Tales*, p. 87.
12 *Cottage Tales*, p. 18.
13 *Cottage Tales*, p. 99.
14 John Clare, *The Shepherd's Calendar*, ed. by Tim Chilcott (Manchester: Carcanet, 2006), p. 11.
15 The scanning system and terminology used here follow Derek Attridge, *The Rhythms of English Poetry* (London: Routledge, 1982).
16 *Cottage Tales*, p. 73.
17 *Cottage Tales*, p. 19.
18 *Cottage Tales*, p. 22.
19 Stancek, 'Lyric Ear', p. 6.
20 Bernard Capp, *When Gossips Meet: Women, Family and Neighbourhood in Modern England* (Oxford University Press, 2007), p. 57.
21 Capp, *When Gossips Meet*, p. 268.
22 Adam Fox, *Oral and Literate Culture in England, 1500-1700* (Oxford University Press, 2000), p. 175 quoted in Goodridge, 'Storytellings: "Old Women's Memorys"', p. 169.
23 Stancek, 'Lyric Ear', p. 5.
24 Fiona Stafford, *Reading Romantic Poetry* (Chichester: Wiley-Blackwell, 2014), pp. 132-61 (p. 150).
25 *Cottage Tales*, p. 9.
26 Stancek, 'Lyric Ear', xi.
27 Stancek, 'Lyric Ear', xii.
28 *Early Poems*, II, pp. 123-79 (p. 128).
29 The concept is initially theorised by Coleridge in his *Biographia Literaria* (1817) but runs through the works of many Romantic writers. See for instance 'Fancy' by John Keats, first published in *Lamia, Isabella, The Eve of St. Agnes, and Other Poems* (1820): 'Ever let the Fancy roam, / Pleasure never is at home […].' *Keats's Poetry and Prose*, ed. by Jeffrey N. Cox (New York: Norton, 2008), p. 465.
30 Stafford, 'Reading or Listening: Romantic Voices', p. 135.
31 William Wordsworth, *The Poems of William Wordsworth. Volume I: Collected Reading Texts from the Cornell Wordsworth*, ed. by Jared R Curtis, 3rd edition, 3 vols (Humanities-Ebooks, LLP, 2014), I, p. 657.
32 Stafford, *Reading Romantic Poetry*, p. 132.
33 Stafford, *Reading Romantic Poetry*, p. 134.
34 Stancek, 'Lyric Ear', p. x.
35 Susan Stewart, *Poetry and the Fate of the Senses* (University of Chicago Press, 2002), p. 110.

'Alauda arvensis. Sky-Lark', (1862-1873). Rare Book Division, The New York Public Library Digital Collections.

John Clare and the Shifting Skylark
Sam Hickford and Em Challinor

Clare repeatedly returns to the skylark as a source both of poetic inspiration and as a natural historical subject. He maintains a relationship in both verse and prose with this common lark that comfortably spans three decades and bridges Clare's role as an agrarian labourer with his time in asylums. In this article, we want to investigate the skylark as a fluid component of Clare's verse, examining various poems Clare either ostensibly addresses or dedicates specifically to the skylark or in which he otherwise references the skylark. Such analysis will hopefully interrogate how the skylark's symbolic resonances shift throughout Clare's verse: the skylark is originally grounded, indelibly tied to empirical observation, but becomes decentred during Clare's time in Northampton Asylum. We will therefore complicate two apparently opposing readings centered on one of Clare's skylark poems (entitled 'The Skylark' in 1835's *The Rural Muse)* published in Clare's mid-career. Namely, we will suggest that P.M.S Dawson's idea that the skylark serves as the 'figure of the poet' and W. John Coletta's idea that Clare's skylark involves the 'semiosis of nature' and a resistance to the 'transcendentals' of 'big science' do not fully capture the complexity of Clare's response to the early nineteenth century trend for skylark-orientated poetry.[1] This focus on the skylark will hopefully help to challenge a critical tendency to view Clare's references to individual bird species as comprehensive, stable, and easy to summarise.

In order to understand Clare's own relationship to this aforementioned trend, it is necessary to provide a brief account of the skylark's metamorphosis as a poetic symbol during the early nineteenth century. The inception of the bird as an exclusively poetic image appears in William Wordsworth's 1807 poem 'To a Sky-Lark', published in the first volume of *Poems in two volumes, and other poems: 1800-1807.* By the 1820s and 1830s, the skylark had been adopted as a metaphor for both peripatetic weariness and transcendence almost to the point of a cliché.[2] Wordsworth developed this ornithological symbol, however, from his engagement with natural history.

When considering late eighteenth and early nineteenth century literary culture, indeed, we must acknowledge that natural history was not neatly separate from literary criticism. In his 1776 work, *British Zoology,* Thomas Pennant provides empirical measurements for the skylark, and elaborates upon its 'reddish brown' colour, but also describes it emotively, stating that, 'it will often soar to such a height, that we are charmed with the music when we lose sight of the songster'.[3] In a further apparent conflation of genres jarring for modern readers, Pennant then states that, 'Milton, in his *Allegro,* most beautifully expresses these circumstances'. For Pennant, in lines like 'To hear the lark begin his flight / And singing startle the dull night', Milton is invoking for us 'the regularity of his life, and the innocence of his own mind'. In other words, Milton's reference to the skylark allows the reader to imagine his own diligent, quasi-monastic morning routine, particularly attuned to bird-song, and Pennant judges that speculating thus on how skylarks function in poetry is fitting for a work of 'zoology'.[4] After venturing this perceptive literary criticism, Pennant reverts to observations on the skylark's colour pattern and its nests among 'clod'.

Wordsworth visited Pennant during his 1790 tour of Snowdonia, having read Pennant's *A Tour in* Wales.[5] Wordsworth's 1807 'To a Sky-Lark' can be seen as incorporating this fluid style of natural history into versification, as well as reworking the skylark as a figure within the peripatetic *Poems in Two Volumes,* a wayfarer on Wordsworth's exhaustive tour. This is made plain when we consider that 'To a Sky-lark' is featured in a section subtitled, 'During a tour, chiefly on foot'. It is preceded by a poem about an idealised female beggar – a 'weed of glorious feature', who meets her unfortunate end – and succeeded by an ode to the moon.[6] Wordsworth's skylark is one of many figures, human and non-human, who Wordsworth dramatises as making a strong impression on him during his tour of the British Isles. When Wordsworth's speaker states there is 'joy divine / In that song of thine', for example, the skylark could be something as similarly distant and unknowable as the moon, and Wordsworth deploys the skylark within traditional symbolic framework.

There is a slightly more earthy tone when the skylark is figured as a companion to an unexplained peregrination and a rousing call for the addressee, then speaker, to continue this journey. In this way, it could be regarded as an *aubade*, with the skylark's song beginning with two dactyls ('Up with me! Up with me!') that the speaker translates into an iambic injunction to continue ('I on the earth will go plodding on'.[7]) Combined with this resolve to look downwards, we see a direct influence from natural history writers like Pennant when Wordsworth considers that the skylark does nest somewhere imprecise but grounded, and outside of a transcendental realm ('Thou hast a nest for thy love and thy rest'[8]). There is a tension, then, in Wordsworth's 1807 skylark: the skylark is both a real bird and a cosmic force in endless transcendental rapture, 'pouring out praise to the Almighty Giver'.[9]

When Percy Shelley adopted the skylark as a symbol for sudden transcendence, he largely eschewed natural history, focusing instead on the symbolic aspects of the skylark. In publishing his 'To a Sky-lark' in June 1820, in conjunction with *Prometheus Unbound*, Shelley is invoking classical tropes in which birds are mythic figures, tropes that Wordsworth had wished to move beyond in his 1807 poem. Mary Shelley informs us that the poem was inspired by a real encounter with a skylark. She records that she and Percy heard the skylark 'carolling' among 'myrtle hedges' during a 'stroll' – invoking leisure (contrasting with Wordsworth's more Herculean 'tours') in Livorno, Italy.[10] Shelley's poem, however, could have been about virtually any bird less common than a house sparrow: the arbitrary choice of the skylark is driven by a desire to craft a Platonic image. While there are no explicit references to Plato, Stewart Wilcox's statement that the poem largely invokes the skylark as a Platonic ideal seems sensible when we consider that Shelley addresses the skylark as an ephemeral bird that 'never wert', as a 'cloud of fire', as 'Sprite or Bird', 'Poet', and even as necessarily immortal given it is contrasted with what we 'mortals dream'.[11] Even though focused on transcendence, Shelley's poem is still made possible by natural history's descriptions of the skylark, and Shelley's Platonic image still depends upon the skylark as a real presence. Shelley references an exalted moment of hearing the skylark when he positions it 'among the flowers and grasses, which screen it from the view'. In calling the ground-nesting skylark a 'scorner of the ground', however, Shelley definitely indicates that natural history is not quite his primary concern, and that such natural details pinpoint the skylark as an idea more elusive than the actual bird, even something esoteric.[12]

'The Skylark' (1850), Samuel Palmer.
Metropolitan Museum of Art, New York.

Shelley's idea of the Platonic skylark was clearly influential, and after his death in 1822, skylark poetry either implicitly or explicitly referencing Shelley's 1820 'To a Sky-Lark' underwent a revitalised trend. Wordsworth's 1825 poem, 'To a Sky-Lark' certainly implicitly references Shelley's more mystical idea of the skylark when he refers to it as, 'ethereal minstrel! pilgrim of the sky!', and calls it a 'type of the wise who soar, but never roam / true to the kindred points of Heaven and Home!'.[13] Wordsworth's invocation of the skylark as a poetic angel returning to its original realm clearly references and refines Shelley's 1820 poem. Wordsworth also wishes to preserve the sense of natural historical detail that is sacrificed in Shelley's rhapsodic mode, however, even if this is always integrated with more fanciful poetic diction: he refers to 'thy nest upon the dewy ground! / Thy nest which thou canst drop into at will'.[14] Felicia Hemans' 1832 poem 'The Swan and the Skylark' explicitly references Shelley's poem. A dying swan converses with a joyous skylark, bidding him 'sing through the echoing sky!' in metrically uneven quatrains.[15] The poem is elegiac, figuratively commemorating Shelley's death, even if it commemorates this obliquely through an ornithological conversation: it carries an epigraph from Shelley's 'To a Sky-Lark'.

It is an associative minefield originating in Wordsworth and renewed by Shelley that Clare must navigate as both a natural historian, a poet, a diligent reader of poetry, and a rural labourer. In an 1825 journal entry, Clare records 'hear[ing] the skylark sing at Swordy well'.[16] This simple record shows Clare's quotidian familiarity with the skylark: he does not record an exalted encounter with this bird in Livorno, or on an expansive tour, but upon a limestone quarry, a familiar local landmark. Clare was also familiar with Pennant's ornithological works, such as his *Genera of Birds*, and at one point records his friend, Edmund Artis, scouring this work upon his request.[17] Sticking to local associations, Clare associates the skylark with cornfields, rather than exotic locations. In a poem composed in the early 1830s, 'The Shepherd's Song', the skylark emerges from its habitat in a timely fashion to accompany a wedding ceremony: 'see yonder skylark from the corn / rises to sing his wedding lay.'[18]

It is this quotidian familiarity that Clare consecrates in 'The Skylark', published a decade later in *The Rural Muse*. It can be supposed that Clare had traveled to Swordy Well to record wildlife, but 'The Skylark' relates the work of a truly virtuoso ornithologist.

It dramatises an accidental encounter with a skylark, upon a cornfield, apparently while the speaker is actually supposed to be seriously engaged in the process of tillage, employing the new and disruptive technology of harrowing-machines. This record of an unintentional spot outside of intentional contemplation differs markedly from Shelley and Wordsworth, and creates vastly different effects. Fundamentally, Clare's speaker understands from direct observation that he is implicated in the near destruction of the skylark's habitat. The explicit reference to a mechanistic, agrarian setting is evoked in the first two rhyming couplets:

> ABOVE the russet clods, the corn is seen
> Sprouting its spiry points of tender green,
> Where squats the hare, to terrors wide awake,
> Like some brown clod the harrows failed to break.[19]

Much has been written about the way Clare suppresses the lyrical 'I' in his poetic work, such as Paul Farley's perceptive comment that Clare 'often excelled at getting himself out of the way.'[20] Here, however, we begin with Clare out of the way - the passive voice ('the corn is seen') is incomplete, leading us to speculate on exactly who has seen the corn. It makes most sense to consider that it is the skylark itself. This marks a departure from Wordsworth, who begins with the skylark addressing his speaker, thereby immediately inserting himself in the poem. Here, we instead begin with a visual image, the skylark searching for nourishment. Clare then leads us to other creatures that a new focus on higher yields would glance over. Among the sensitive 'tender green', soon subject to mechanistic action, the hare is subject to terrors 'wide awake'. These hard consonants (/d/, /k/) convey the disrupting force of new ploughing technologies, and their irreverence of the creatures that their aggressive motion ploughs over.

Clare is commenting upon the unobserved challenges to birdlife that are created by new winnowing-machines, that disrupt the whole surface of the soil and therefore cause unprecedented threats to ornithological habitat, such as the skylark's home. These winnowing-machines, able to separate grain from chaff by an 'artificial current of air', had been patented in 1797 by W. S. Dix. In an 1802 encyclopedia, A. F. M. Willich had celebrated the 'increase of produce' generated by such machines.[21] In these first two couplets, Clare pinpoints that, from the perspective of such technologies, the hare in the cornfield is subsumed into human use-value. All of this serves as *mise en scène* to establish where the skylark itself lives: Clare has not depicted the sky yet. Clare has carefully established a fragile pastoral, with humans mechanistically at war with their own ecosystem. As a reputation of transcendence, it has more in common with Wordsworth's 1807 poem than Shelley's more recent intervention, intentionally reviving and emphasising Wordsworth's fleeting engagement with natural history.

Given this poem is composed in rhyming couplets in fairly regular iambic pentameter, it has a lot in common with the sonnets that Seamus Heaney refers to as 'wound up' like 'clockwork'.[22] The poem is not a sonnet, however: it is a continuous stanza of 26 lines in iambic pentameter rhyming couplets. In this sense, it goes beyond Clare's bird sonnets in recalling the iambic pentameter heroic couplets of Alexander Pope and John Dryden that were influential models in much of eighteenth century verse. This legacy would have been apparent in the 1830s, and early nineteenth century readers must have been familiar with Pope's *Pastorals*. Pope evoked the corn harvest in 'Summer: Or Alexis', where the besotted Alexis awaits the time 'when weary reapers quit the sultry field, / And, crown'd with corn, their thanks to Ceres yield.'[23] In using a similar form, Clare is evoking agriculture as something not necessarily as harmonious as 'clockwork', but rather as mechanistic in a more sinister way, establishing a jarring contrast with this more classical, less earthy, manner of pastoral.

Clare uses a slightly less rigid iambic pentameter, however, offset with lines beginning with trochees. The fifth line evokes buttercups 'opening their golden caskets to the sun'. This is both a vivid and a funereal image: the buttercups are both in motion ('opening) and static images of mourning ('caskets'). The commencing trochee ('opening') creates an atmosphere of rupture. It is only after establishing interconnected, terrestrial flora and fauna that Clare even ventures to describe the skylark. Unlike Wordsworth and Shelley, he situates the skylark from the ground upwards, resisting the recent literary impetus to make it an isolated object of reverence, or transcendence:

> Up from their hurry see the Skylark flies
> And o'er her half- formed nest, with happy wings
> Winnows the air, till in the cloud she sings,
> Then hangs a dust spot in the sunny skies,
> And drops, and drops, till in her nest she lies,
> Which they unheeded passed [24]

The skylark, rather than 'divine', is labouring, in the process of constructing a nest. Rather than effortlessly soaring, the action of flight is also a process of mechanistic labour rather than an ecstatic effortlessness ('winnows'). The identification with the skylark as a 'poet' or 'minstrel' still occurs, but, for Clare, this must occur in the process of constructing the bird as a fellow labouring-class poet. In this way, the skylark's flight is not to an imaginary Platonic realm, but downward. In Clare, the preposition 'up' is carefully embedded within a structure, rather than initiating the poem as an imperative, as in Wordsworth. This preposition also occurs in a more laboured, less exalted syntactical pattern ('up from their hurry see the skylark flies'), which we can imagine delivered in an educative tone, as if Clare's speaker has seen all this before and tells the addressee about it only begrudgingly, with a certainty they can not understand the relationships Clare conveyed. We can imagine that other skylark-poets like Wordsworth and Shelley are also 'unheed[ing]' of the skylark's actual habitat.

Nonetheless, while the sense of the skylark's divinity is not emphasised, Clare leaves some room for transcendence. While the skylark is threatened by our 'hurry', and is itself 'hurry[ing]', Clare does imagine 'heavens' as an emancipatory realm:

> Had they the wing
> Like such a bird, themselves would be too proud,
> And build on nothing but a passing cloud!
> As free from danger, as the heavens are free
> From pain and toil, there would they build, and be,
> And sail about the world to scenes unheard
> Of and unseen, — O were they but a bird![25]

In other words, Clare wants us to know that being a skylark is much more challenging than leisurely poets could imagine. Nonetheless, the 'heavens' are still figured as 'free / from pain and toil', even though this is in the context of Clare's acerbic thought-experiment, imagining that poets or artists knew the hardships of being a bird first-hand. A transcendent heavenly sphere is still present, even if it is not as easy as it looks to fly into it. Clare is emphasising with a competitive edge that he empathises with birds more keenly, because he understands a little more what being a skylark actually entails. The poem ends by reiterating this nuanced position. The poets listen to the skylark's song: 'While its low nest, moist with the dews of morn, / Lies safely, with the leveret, in the corn'.²⁶ Clare, here, wants to repeatedly emphasise that the skylark is a ground-nesting bird, and that as a grounded poet, he is close to it. His class status is weaponised into a poetic advantage. There could also be something sly about this ending: unlike other poets, he knows where the skylark lives, next to the vulnerable but resilient hare. It is readily possible to mediate between Dawson and Coletta's readings and aver that Clare is both emphasising his identification with the skylark, and attempting to depict the complex ecological relationships that sustain it.

Clare focuses on the skylark's nest, rather than its flight or song, in another mid-career poem, 'The Skylark Leaving Her Nest'. This was not included in The Rural Muse, though it does appear in The Midsummer Cushion manuscripts. Unlike the more unstable single stanza of 'The Skylark', this poem is in the sculpted quatrains that Laura Betz has associated with 'hidden spaces', or textual sanctuary, in a 2024 essay.²⁷ This poem has a little more room for the visionary, even if the skylark is emphasised as flying away from its surprisingly flimsy home, rather than soaring *ex nihilo* into transcendent flight:

> To see thee with a sudden start
>   The green and placid herbage leave
>   And in mid-air a vision weave
>   For joy's delighted heart²⁸

Clare's verbal choice is interesting here: the vision, like a nest, is 'woven', arrived at by intricate labour. This foreshadows the manner in which the skylark becomes an even more complex symbol in Clare's later work. Numerous complexities put Clare at a remove from these two mid-career skylark-poems. After his institutionalisation in Northampton Asylum, Clare lived in a town and was largely confined indoors. His identity as a rural poet was jeopardised: he was less able to capitalise upon the rightful pride he had assumed in pointing out the skylark's actual nest. Additionally, Clare wasn't writing for publication, and therefore had lost the print audience he had enjoyed as the 'Northamptonshire Peasant Poet'. Clare likely only had William Knight, a fellow verse-writer and the house-steward at Northampton Asylum, by way of an audience. It is certainly clear that Clare struggled to write about subjects that had previously caught his attention. Clare complained to Knight that, 'I would try like the Birds a few songs i' the Spring but they have shut me up'.²⁹

It seems equally clear, however, that part of Clare still wanted to write about these subjects, and that Knight encouraged him to do so as a therapeutic exercise, in line with the asylum's commitment to at least pretend to be dedicated to the 'moral treatment' of its patients. In the introduction to Knight's transcripts of Clare, for example, Knight bemoans that, 'whenever I have wished him to correct a single stanza he has shown the greatest disinclination.'[30] It is clear that 'correct[ing]' Clare is both a literary and psychological exercise, and that such correction presumably involves recuperating Clare's identity as a rural poet, convincing him that he can still write about birds.[31] It is not inconceivable that Knight wanted to convince Clare to turn to birds, rather than, for example, Mary, or Lord Byron, as a more accepted means of processing his institutionalisation.

It is with this therapeutic context in mind that we move to two poems written in the mid-1840s. Both poems are entitled 'The Skylark' in the Knight Transcripts. It seems probable, given the preponderance of untitled manuscripts in Clare's later work, that Knight had suggested this title as a means of enhancing the relationship to Clare's pre-institutional work. In this way, and in these neat transcriptions of Clare's pencil manuscripts, Knight is perhaps attempting to accord dignity to Clare's later work, or to clean it up. While out of step with poetic conventions of the time, we might question if Clare's later work needs this dignity, or grooming. In one later 'The Skylark', Clare innovates significantly in terms of the metrical schemes he employs, creating a sestet form that features lines that apparently resemble tetrameter, but actually seem to consist of lines with three beats each. Clare's earlier statement to John Taylor that he had composed 'Song' from the measures of his 'mother's wheel' recalls Clare's capacity for creating lines organised by beat.[32]

'The Skylark' is a reflection on Clare's institutionalisation. The skylark is a common contributor to the dawn chorus, which Clare could have heard from Northampton Asylum. While Northampton in the mid nineteenth century was significantly less built up than Northampton today, the town experienced unprecedented population growth after 1841 as a 'medium-sized light industrial town', according to a 2017 doctoral thesis by Frank Clifford German.[33] Such industrialisation was likely to have exerted a significant effect on bird populations. Clare presumably did not have significant time to wander, and from his common perch at St.

Ann's Church, it must have been vastly more difficult to observe the skylark than it had been in previous deindustrialised locations, like Swordy Well.[34] While Clare presumably did hear the skylark, then, he nonetheless continues to imaginatively associate it with cornfields, perhaps given this is where he more clearly observed it:

> Although I am in prison
>   Thy song is uprisen
> And singing away to the cloud
>   In the blueness of morn
>   Over fields of green corn
>   With a song sweet rural and loud[35]

The 'fields of green corn' is certainly a pluralised reference to the 1835 'The Skylark', but the memory of this poem also seems distorted. Clare does not recall the acerbic tone of this poem, protesting the 'heedless[ness]' of those who avoid the skylark's nest, but instead recalls the 'song sweet rural and loud'. This can be explained by a kind of wistfulness, with Clare retracing the contours of his memory and drawing a newly hopeful message from contemplating the skylark's song. The cornfields he remembers still exist, even if he is displaced. This displacement is emphasised through the skylark. Clare continues to adopt the skylark as a figure for himself, but must now reconcile his lack of clear visual contact with the skylark by offering an image of the skylark, like himself, more fully leaving its nest: 'On the earth's grassy nest / Thou has left thy brown nest.'[36] Instead, the skylark must now depend upon hospitality, with Clare concluding the fifth sestet with the five-beat line, 'And of each grassy close thou'rt the poet and guest'.[37] As the poem progresses, the sestets become more interspersed with five-beat lines, with this newly-created fluid metrical scheme emphasising Clare's newly-found unrootedness.

In attempting to recreate an empirical observation from memory, Clare is compelled to adopt a more visionary mode, a departure from the groundedness of the 1835 'The Skylark' and the clarity of 'The Skylark Leaving Her Nest'. Clare does supply natural historical details, such as describing the skylark's 'brown russet wing'.[38] Clare is forced to depart, however, from what Stephanie Kuduk Weiner describes as his 'mimesis' of nature, and contend with a Shelleyan visionary poetics in the absence of a thorough empirical observation to dramatise.[39] Thus, Clare describes the skylark's song 'like a vision begun / of pleasure and lonely delight', indicating he is definitively reconciled to the 'fancy' he earlier decried.[40] This visionary poetics occurs also at an acoustic level. Clare more often uses pararhymes, such as the opening pararhyme ('prison / uprisen'). This is an ingenious rhyme, signalling that the two near antonyms are nonetheless nearly homophones. The rhyme scheme of AABCCB facilitates this loose, associative flow of perfect rhymes and pararhymes.

Another poem called 'The Skylark' in the Knight Transcripts marks a further merging of Shelleyan visionary poetics with natural historical detail, mirroring Wordsworth while retaining a distinctly Clarean poetics. In this poem, the skylark apparently transcends the cornfields that Clare had earlier associated with it. Rather than just flying to a disembodied realm, however, the skylark surveys recognisable features of landscape. Clare creates another new stanzaic form at the service of this visionary and naturalistic poetry, a quatrain pattern alternating between lines of approximately twelve syllables and shorter lines of eight or ten syllables:

> O'er grass ground and plough'd fields now whistles the sky lark
> Oer fallow field meadow and glen
> Oer moist moors and furze heaths oer Paddock and dry park
> It whistles its ditty springs coming agen[41]

The lack of punctuation signifies the skylark's abrupt flight, but Clare is still eager to tell us that the skylark passes above complex habitats ('furze heath', 'moist moors') in its flight. Clare also later includes the skylark's 'copple crown', and tells us that it 'sits on its nest', as if to indicate he knows it is still more than a Platonic abstraction.[42] Clare must consider the skylark beyond its nest, however, in line with his awareness of having been plucked from his own nest. The skylark's flight here is imaginary, or even hallucinatory, a metaphor perhaps for Clare's interior experience and a release from his psychological problems. Conceiving of ecstatic flight becomes a way to conceive of landscapes beyond his own entrapment.

As the skylark's nest becomes less visible in Northampton Asylum, Clare must conceive of the skylark beyond it, even though his ability to locate its nest was what had driven him to poeticise it in his mid-career work. This always necessarily involves a more thorough turn towards the visionary that he had been cautious of in his earlier work, and a greater focus on mere linguistic play rather than empirical poetics. The rhyme of 'sky lark' and 'dry park' embodies such linguistic play, as does the odd verbal construction 'whistles its ditty springs', which seems to be missing an infinitive (like 'to herald') and uses 'ditty' unconventionally as an adjective. Clare is distorting pastoral lexis, creating new grammatical structures to render it unfamiliar, to convey his own disordered psychological state.

In Clare's later work, then, the skylark mutates into an emotional reality, a generalised presence. In other words, it becomes a symbol, as well as the same ground-nesting bird. This is apparent in Clare's reference to the skylark in an untitled hymnodic poem, '[Love hearken the skylark]'. It is most apparent, however, in a poem called 'Mary: A Ballad' (which was also elsewhere titled 'Jessy: A Ballad'). The poem is in an acatalectic tetrameter construction that, in its rigidity, appears designed to be disorientating, as if the metre is trying to maintain an artificial stability. This is the same atmosphere as another poem written during Clare's institutionalisation, one of Clare's poems titled 'Glinton Spire' that begins, 'I love to see the slender spire'.[43] Here, the skylark begins the poem as a certainty, an assured presence: 'The skylark mounts up with the morn / the valleys are green with the spring'.[44] It is as if Clare is in the process of creating a hallucinatory Arcadia, that defies the walls of the asylum. In creating this Arcadia, however, he is not able to visualise Mary: 'But Mary can never be seen / Though she all chasing spring doth begin'.[45] Clare then betrays his artistic intentions and his rationale for writing. Picturing the skylark song was an attempt to conjure Mary: 'the birds almost whistle her name / Say where can my Mary be gone'.[46] This dramatises the shift I have described most acutely. The skylark was originally a proud symbol of Clare's actual connection to the land. It is now, relatedly, a talisman, a means of conjuring lost memories. As something Clare can still hear but no longer fully see, it is a partial but ultimately imperfect gateway into an authentic, lost rural past. In following Clare's skylark, we follow Clare's unique voyage towards the imaginative realm, where the empirical or mimetic is nonetheless always still clung to.

NOTES

1. W. John Coletta, '"Writing larks": John Clare's Semiosis of Nature', *Wordsworth Circle*, XXVIII:3 (Summer 1997), 192-200 (p. 192). P. M. S. Dawson, 'Of Birds and Bards: Clare and his Romantic Contemporaries', *John Clare: New Approaches* ed. by John Goodridge and Simon Kövesi (Peterborough: John Clare Society, 2000), pp. 149-59 (p. 157).
2. William Wordsworth, 'To a Sky-Lark', *Poems in Two Volumes, and Other Poems: 1800-1807* (Ithaca, New York: Cornell University Press, 1973), p. 117.
3. Thomas Pennant, *British Zoology* (Warrington: B. White, 1776), p. 353.
4. Ibid., p. 354.
5. Jonathan Bate, *Radical Wordsworth: The Poet Who Changed The World* (London: William Collins, 2020), p. 85.
6. Wordsworth, 'Beggars', *Poems in Two Volumes*, p. 114, stanza 3, l. 6 and p. 118.
7. Wordsworth, 'To a Sky-Lark', *Poems in Two Volumes*, p. 118, stanza 2, l. 21.
8. Ibid., stanza 2, l. 11.
9. Ibid., stanza 2, l. 17.
10. Grylls Glynn, *Mary Shelley* (Oxford University Press, 1938), p. 121.
11. Percy Shelley, 'To a Sky-lark', *Shelley's Skylark: Facsimile of the Original Manuscript* (Cambridge, MA: Library of Harvard University, 1888), stanza 1, l. 2; stanza 2, l. 3; stanza 13, l. 1; stanza 8, l. 1; stanza 17, l. 5; stanza 20, l. 5. Shelley alters 'the' to 'a' in the manuscript – perhaps indicating that he is moving away from describing the non-Platonic skylark. See Stewart C. Wilcox, 'The Sources, Symbolism, and Unity of Shelley's "Skylark"', *Studies in Philology* 46:4 (1949), 560-76.
12. Percy Shelley, 'To a Sky-lark', stanza 10, l. 5; stanza 20, l. 5.
13. William Wordsworth, 'To a Sky-lark', *The Poems of William Wordsworth* (London: Edward Moxon, 1858), p. 162, stanza 1, l. 1; stanza 2, ll. 5-6.
14. Ibid., stanza 3, ll. 2-3.
15. Felicia Hemans, 'The Swan and the Skylark', *The Poems of Felicia Hemans* (London: W.P. Nimmo, 1875), p. 552, stanza 11, l. 4.
16. *By Himself*, p. 213.
17. *By Himself*, p. 236.
18. Clare, 'The Shepherd's Song', in *The Poems of John Clare* (London: J. M. Dent, 1935), p. 75.
19. Clare, 'The Skylark', *The Rural Muse* (London: Whittaker, 1835), p. 83.
20. Paul Farley, 'Introduction', *John Clare* (London: Faber and Faber, 2007), p. xii.
21. A. F. M. Willich, *The Domestic Encyclopedia* (London: Murray and Highley, 1802), pp. 338-9.
22. Seamus Heaney, 'John Clare's Prog', in *The Redress of Poetry* (London: Faber and Faber, 1995), p. 78.
23. Alexander Pope, 'Summer: Or Alexis', *Pastorals* (London: Nicholson and Co., 1793), pp. 70-1.
24. Clare, 'The Skylark', *The Rural Muse*, p. 83.
25. Ibid..
26. Ibid., pp. 25-6.
27. Laura Betz, 'John Clare's Sonnets as Nests', *JCSJ*, 43 (2024), 5.
28. Clare, 'The Skylark Leaving Her Nest', *The Poems of John Clare* (London: J.M. Dent, 1935), p. 294, stanza 3.

29. Arthur Foss, *St Andrew's Hospital: The First 150 Years* (Cambridge: Granta Editions, 1988), p. 136.
30. William Knight, Introduction to Northampton Library Manuscript (hereafter NMS) 1 (1).
31. NMS 1 (1).
32. Letter to John Taylor, 11 May 1820, *Letters*, p. 65.
33. Frank Clifford German, 'Migration, work and housing in Northampton: 1841-1871' (unpublished doctoral thesis, University College London, 2017).
34. Based on field work by Em Challinor, Northampton, April 2024.
35. Clare, 'The Skylark', stanza 1, NMS 1 (42).
36. NMS 1 (42).
37. NMS 1 (42).
38. NMS 1 (42).
39. Stephanie Kuduk Weiner, *Clare's Lyric* (Oxford University Press, 2014), p. 2.
40. NMS 1 (42).
41. Clare, 'The Skylark', NMS 2 (192).
42. NMS 2 (192).
43. Clare, 'Glinton Spire', Peterborough Manuscript A54, p. 380v, l. 1.
44. Clare, 'Mary: A Ballad', NMS 1 (235).
45. NMS 1 (235).
46. NMS 1 (235).

'Shepherdess Resting (Noon)' (19th century), Jean-François Millet.
Harvard Art Museums/Fogg Museum, Gift of Edward M. M. Warburg.

WHEN BEASTS SPOKE

Charlotte Strawbridge Art

A collection of illustrated thoughts from some wise beings with important things to tell us...

From the animal's perspective, these thoughts inspire contemplation on some big ideas, in gentle short stories. From lessons on mindfulness, self-love, and gratitude, to observations on the little things and the joys of nature.

Once upon a time, when beasts spoke and people were silent, there was a valley so deeply full of love that all the beings in the world knew of its magic. Each leaf had been gently blessed, each tree was rooted in ancient wisdom, and the valley was entirely covered in woodland. Little creatures roamed the land to learn of love and all its wonders.

Original Canvases | Fine Art Prints | Thoughtful Gifts

www.charlottestrawbridge.co.uk

Reviews

The Edinburgh Edition of the Works of Allan Ramsay, Volumes 2-3. By ALLAN RAMSAY; *Poems 1721 & 1728* and *Poems, Uncollected and Dubia*, ed. Rhona Brown. Edinburgh: Edinburgh University Press, 2023. Pp. xxi+76, i+449 (two volumes). £200.00 (hardback).

John Clare seems to have got his first real taste of Scottish poetry from Allan Ramsay (1686-1758). When he first planned a book of poetry, 'A Rustic's Pastime, In Leisure Hours', in 1814, he mocked up a title-page for it, using nine lines from one of Ramsay's verse epistles as an epigraph for this imagined book, beginning 'Some like to laugh their time away, / To dance while pipes or fiddles play, / And have nae sense of ony want / As lang as they can drink or rant' (*Early Poems*, I, p. 3; Ramsay, Vol. 2, pp. 202-4). When critics, a few years later, complained about his 'too frequent imitations of Burns', he protested that when his first poems were written he knew nothing of Burns, but 'I had an odd volume of Ramsay a long while and if I imitated any it should be him to which I am ready to acknowledge a great deal' (*By Himself*, p. 115). Ramsay would ultimately be eclipsed in Clare's pantheon by Burns, as he was within Scottish literary culture. Yet he remained a foundational figure in vernacular poetry, and Clare would maintain his interest: when Sir Walter Scott sent Clare's publishers a gift of money to buy the poet books, Clare asked for and received a new edition of Ramsay (*Letters*, pp. 51, 57). He ultimately owned volume I of Ramsay's *Poems on Several Occasions* (1793)—this was his 'odd volume'—and Ramsay's *Poems* (1819), including a biography of the poet by William Tennant. These volumes both survive among his books in Northamptonshire Central Library. (Thanks to Dean Goldsmith at the Library for checking them).

Clare would have found in Ramsay's work a groundedness and an accessibility. He would have enjoyed the textures of the Doric language, perhaps taking some inspiration for resisting London-centred, standardised English. He would have noted Ramsay's interest in song and folk culture. The satires and elegies would have been read carefully. Ramsay offered a distinctive style of pastoral, set in a Scottish landscape that must have fed Clare's lifelong interest in the distant northern land of his absent paternal grandfather. The poetry's formal and thematic variety and its lively sociability would be further attractions to a young poet looking for ways of representing his own world. He would not have failed to note Ramsay's frequent topicality, or his bouncing confidence, a remarkable self-belief as a poet. Also important to the growth of Clare's own confidence as a poet would be the essential cheeriness of Ramsay, his largely good-humoured tone (the epigraphic quotation includes the lines, 'May I be happy in my lays / Is all my wish'). While charming verse epistles to patrons such as Sir John Clerk might also have suggested strategies for Clare's approaches to his own, often difficult, patron relationships.

If Ramsay remains too little known nowadays (certainly compared to his world-famous successor), this new multi-volume library edition

'Dilapidated Cottage with Sleeping Peasant and Three Women Spinning' (17th century), Abraham Bloemaert (1566-1651). The Maida and George Abrams Collection, Fogg Art Museum, Harvard University.

may well help change the situation. It replaces the old six-volume Scottish Text Society edition, whose painful defects and lack of co-ordination reflect its protracted birth (disrupted by a world war, among other things). The new Edinburgh edition, headed by a strong team from the University of Glasgow led by Murray Pittock, is better focused and organised, and much more ambitious, taking an active interest in all aspects of the poet's work and its context, including his editing and collecting of poems and songs, his music, his drama, his textual and publishing complexity, and his social and cultural context including rural and city worlds; also such vital scholarly desiderata as a new bibliography, to encompass the many and varied publications of a poet whose editor calls him a 'true cultural polymath' (Vol. 2, p. 1)—the edition's general editor calls Ramsay 'a fox rather than a hedgehog: someone good at many things' (Vol. 2, p. v). Outside the texts, the production of the edition has been accompanied by much supportive activity, including Ramsay Festivals and the development of 'Ramsay Trails' in Edinburgh and elsewhere. If the world fails to rediscover Ramsay in a big way, it won't be from lack of diligent effort on the part of this team.

The present, two-volume segment of the Edinburgh edition gathers in his poems, both the two main selections he published in the 1720s (Vol. 2) and a sweeping-up of uncollected poems and odds and ends (Vol. 3). It offers a cornucopia of riches, giving a sense of Ramsay's range and development as a poet. This is a first rate edition, well up to the high standards of the first Volume, *The Shepherd's Calendar* (reviewed in the *European Romantic Review*, 34, no. 4 (2023), pp. 501-4). It is clear and comprehensive in its presentation and apparatus, and is completed by a biography, glossary, textual and general annotation, a bibliography, and indexes. The two principal editions of 1721 and 1728 are kept as they first appeared in terms of preliminaries, subscription lists, etc., which takes one close to the poet's initial sense of self-presentation. And the two volumes are very well introduced by the editor, Rhona Brown, who contextualises the poetry, dealing with its challenging bibliographical complexity including numerous single-poem publications and a fair amount of 'bootlegs' and other oddities, and examining, too, the ways in which Ramsay achieved his successes, looking at issues such as patronage and routes into print and the marketplace. She summarises Ramsay's key concerns as a poet, as 'the use of the Scots language in literary texts', and 'nuanced neoclassicism, good-natured yet pointed satire, cautious sympathy for the Jacobite cause and the celebration of the ordinary, everyday life of Scotland' (p. 2). Clareans may well wish to request these volumes from their local library, and discover just what excited Clare about this poetry, now that it has been properly edited.

John Goodridge

The Cambridge Companion to John Clare. ed. SARAH HOUGHTON-WALKER. Cambridge: Cambridge University Press, 2024. Pp. xv + 277. £22.99 (paperback).

The *Cambridge Companions to...* series was launched nearly 40 years ago with *Companions* to Shakespeare and Chaucer. The series aims to provide students with overviews of their author or topic that might also prompt new lines of enquiry. It is high time, one might think, that John Clare had a *Companion*. This is a rich gathering of essays that will provide just the guide that students new to Clare will need, expertly edited by Sarah Houghton-Walker. These accessible, relatively brief chapters will prove appealing to many readers of Clare, including but not limited to those under pressure to submit 2000-word essays that contribute to their degree classifications. Indeed, these thoughtful, well-informed chapters will be important reading for seasoned scholars of Clare. They may take the opportunity a collection like this grants to reflect on the shape that John Clare studies presents to the world today.

The book is divided into four parts. The first four chapters consider 'Clare the poet'. That alarmed me at first, but in fact almost all 16 chapters focus principally on Clare's poetry. The next group considers Clare the naturalist. Two chapters explore Clare's poetic accounts of animals and flowers before a chapter on Clare's reading of natural history and a survey of ecocritical approaches to Clare. The third section looks at Clare's image: how he constructed his sense of self, how Clare edited and revised his poetic self-image, and how others envisioned him in visual art. The final section presents five chapters on influence and tradition, taking in religion, labouring-class writing, politics, health, and poetic influence.

These are just the issues that readers new to Clare will benefit from having expert and accessible guidance upon. The authors make things easy for their readers. The writing is clear and accessible, if only occasionally a little twee. Recent scholarship is quietly alluded to rather than densely footnoted. There is a helpful set of appendices: a detailed chronology and a very well selected set of suggestions for further reading.

The book aims to be companionable to the reader new to Clare rather than—as with other recent edited collections on the poet—seeking to push Clare studies down new paths. Nonetheless, the book might be said to present, quietly, an argument, and perhaps even to stage arguments that currently exist among Clare scholars. A strong emphasis is placed on close attention to Clare's poetic processes. Andrew Hodgson is acute on Clare's 'tempered regard for the significance of form' (p. 32) in his reading of the push and pull between looseness and organisation in Clare's poetics. Mark Storey's chapter on Clare's habits of editing and revision should inspire readers to explore the many versions of Clare's poems that are now readily available thanks to the efforts of his editors. Storey reveals a poet who comes alive, creatively, in the process of revision. Chapters by James Castell and Fiona Stafford look, respectively, at Clare's poetic accounts of animals and plants. They are thoughtful, imaginative readings, zooming in on well-chosen examples while also giving a broader survey. Castell's fine observation about the 'hesitations and obscurities' in Clare's encounters with nonhumans that are 'easy to overlook' (p. 80) is characteristic of the book's excellent close readings.

Most of the chapters address in some way Clare's poetics and his interest in the nonhuman world, and I wonder if the book reveals a division among Clare scholars regarding how to read that relationship. Several chapters register what Houghton-Walker calls Clare's 'adaptive appropriation of standard forms and lexicons' (p. 11). Robert Heyes describes what Clare drew from his reading of contemporary natural historians: precision and range of knowledge. That Clare 'was well informed about other parts of the world, including their natural history' (p. 106) is a point that still needs making. Heyes ends by suggesting how this knowledge improved Clare's poetry. Ross Wilson's thoughtful chapter reads Clare in close and complex relation with theorists and poets of the sublime, including Kant and the eighteenth-century reception of Longinus. Fiona Stafford draws out Clare's 'deep knowledge and knowingness' to set against simplistic praise of his 'directness' (p. 103), a facet she brings out by exploring his subtle echoes of Milton, Burns, and Wordsworth.

These chapters give us a knowing, knowledgeable, literary Clare. Others present a different Clare, a poet marked by his closeness to the earth, his refusal of structuring frames of perception, what Tim Chilcott calls a 'direct, unmediated physicality' (p. 137) resistant to abstraction, reading, and visionary flight. For Stephanie Kuduk Weiner, in Clare's lyrics, Clare and the world he describes are 'real and immediate' (p. 22). In Cassandra Falke's account, perception and poetry are barely distinguishable in Clare's poetics of 'receptivity, active and embodied notice-taking' (p. 57). The two sides are there in Mina Gorji's sparkling concluding chapter on Clare's two-way relation with other poets. The second half points to Clare's delighted openness to others' writing. Rather than seeing an untamed Clare rejecting James Thomson's cultured formalism, Gorji shows us the 'textures and sounds' (p. 253) of Thomson's 'freshened world' that Clare echoes. It's a fine end to the collection, but a slightly awkward pairing with the chapter's first half. Here Seamus Heaney and a series of Heaney-esque poets value Clare as a poet of dense, dialect-driven locality, a poet of grounded reality to set in opposition to human artifice.

Scott McEathron's reading of the 'constructed image' of Clare reminds us of the dangers both of the commodification of 'Clare' and the 'moralistic advocacy' (p. 166) that claims to have discovered the 'real Clare'. The *Cambridge Companion* does not do either; instead, the range of chapters suggests the diverse forms that 'John Clare' is beginning to take. The book points towards new paths and new ways of taking old ones. Ecocriticism remains the dominant mode in Clare scholarship, but, as Markus Poetzsch shows in his excellent survey of the field, quite what ecocriticism means is up for debate. Poetzsch notes that Clare scholars, having once set the pace in ecocriticism, have not typically kept up with contemporary interests in the global and complex questions of scale. More common are accounts that emphasise his 'attentive and self-circumscribing mode' (p. 129); the time may be ripe, then, for new kinds of ecocritical Clare.

Emma Mason provides a welcome and insightful reading of Clare's religion, emphasising Clare's Christianity, his career-long interactions with the Bible, and the importance this has for his accounts of the natural world. Bridget Keegan's chapter offers at once a helpful overview and an original perspective in discussing several other labouring-class poets and their interest in emerging ideas of industrial time. Expanding on that, Tim Fulford presents Clare as a poet not of place and nature but of 'dislocation and denaturing' (p. 212), a poet angrily protesting about the iniquities of class-based oppression. Erin Lafford's account of Clare's health is imaginative and fresh in the best tradition of essays for this series. She pushes against the biographical pull of his sad end in the madhouse. Her term, which Clare used of himself, is 'indisposed'. The uncertainty of that condition allows Lafford to rethink such staples of Clare scholarship as locality, class, and embodiment. Clare's desire to feel well makes of him a poet 'frequently on the move' who found, perhaps surprisingly, London's 'perpetual motion' (p. 238) restorative creatively and physically.

That little glimpse of Clare in London suggests some of the Clares that don't appear here. *Cambridge Companions* aspire to be comprehensive, but of course there is a limit to the generosity of publishers and the stamina of readers. You can't do it all. All the same, the roads not taken are suggestive. Houghton-Walker takes the quite reasonable decision to present Clare's texts as they appear in the standard editions, which is to say in their 'primitive' manuscript form. That's sensible, but might a reader new to Clare need a guide to these complex issues? What of Clare and gender and sexuality, or a focus on the many genres he essayed: non-fictional prose, letters, the periodical essay? I missed the Clare who took such delighted interest in print and print culture, the Clare of the *London Magazine* corresponding with figures like Allan Cunningham and George Darley, reading poets like Letitia Elizabeth Landon. Romantic and Victorian studies have never been more global in their interests. Clare has much to say to this, I'm sure, but it's not a side to him that emerges much here. But it is wrong to complain about what a book isn't rather than to celebrate or at least understand what it is. *The Cambridge Companion to John Clare* stresses his creative vitality and his openness to the world. In doing so it will, I hope, encourage new readers to think afresh about how we envision Clare and his 'disorderly divine' writing, connections, and interests.

David Stewart,
Northumbria University

After Clare. By WILLIAM THOMPSON. Nottingham/Leicester: New Walk Editions, 2022. Pp. 24. £5.00 (paperback).

In the concluding chapter of *John Clare: Nature, Criticism and History* (Palgrave Macmillan, 2017) Simon Kövesi states: 'John Clare seems more present than ever in contemporary literary culture'. I'm curious why Clare is uniquely placed among English poets to evoke a continuing range of creative responses. Is it the prescience, lyricism, and accuracy of his writing; his example of perseverance and creativity despite a range of pressures; the painful fusion between his life and work; a combination of factors? He seems to be placed at the centre of a series of dialogues involving artworks, music, sculpture, poetry, fiction, memoir, photography, plays, radio, TV, and film. The latest (but not the last) contribution to this conversation is William Thompson's pamphlet of poems *After Clare*.

For context, the back cover of this pamphlet explains the background to these poems: 'William Thompson was born in Peterborough in 1991, and grew up in and around Helpston, the birthplace of John Clare...Clare towered over the landscape of his youth: the prospect for Thompson, of writing about it in his shadow, was daunting. More recently, however, he has started to see a way of doing so, by telling the truth about what that landscape is like almost 200 years later'. It's a skilful solution, nimbly avoiding the impossible task of trying to fill Clare's boots, while examining the similarities and contemporary differences of a landscape intimately known to both poets.

Half a dozen of these twenty elegant mostly free-verse poems (with a beautiful half-rhymed sonnet on past friendship) feature Clare in some way, either directly addressing him, referring to him, or quoting him. Let's take a closer look at this group of poems, as examples of the original voice in these pages. Thompson's opening poem 'Clare Country' tackles the challenge head on:

> It's true you got here first, that
> you were born
> in a thatched house, that you
> burnt your calories
> by working in the fields

This is immediate, effective poetry. The poet collars Clare (rather than the reader) from the first six words, and draws the reader into his lines.

The second stanza places the 'I', the speaker, centre stage—in implicit answer to 'you'—and opens with the gentlest rebuttal:

> But I knew this ground before I
> knew of you.
> I've inhaled air rising from the
> same flat land,
> pulled pints in the same pub

Thompson decides to 'lay my claim / to see our skies as a big, blank open page'. He's ready for the task that these poems enact. The phrase 'our skies' shows a subtle claiming of kinship, which is further developed in 'Snipe', borrowing Clare's words by opening with an italicised quotation from the start of Clare's poem: *'Lover of swamps / The quagmire overgrown / With hassock-tufts of sedge'* and in the next tercet Thompson replies:

> Well, not quite. Not anymore.
> Now, you find the filled-in
> gravel pits
> and fishing lakes.

This respectful contradiction draws us into a powerful address to the snipe's ways of adapting to a more constrained landscape. Thompson has a keen eye for comparisons:

> Your beak's a knitting needle
> split in two. Each feather
> is a slice of polished marquetry.

The poem 'Tryst' begins with the lines:

> Imagine Clare spreading his coat
> over the uncut hay,
> his trembling hands, Patty's
> nervous laugh

until the poet updates us with 'It's May, 2020', depicting today's lovers in the grounds of Burghley House at the end of the first Covid lockdown. This focus on time and relationships (with

Clare as an apparent subject) is echoed in 'Public House', where the speaker meets his father who has 'left the family home'. The poem circles around Clare's drunkenness, death and burial and a stilted loyalty between father and son, as if all three men might be emblems of a troubled masculinity. Physical closeness feels forbidden in this version of men:

> Light makes it through St
>   Botolph's yew.
> My dad looks out. And I don't
>   think I hold his hand.

In 'United Reformed Church' Clare makes a surprise appearance at an AA Meeting. It's an appealing portrait, a meshing of time-zones, almost like a posthumous admission from Clare about his problems, an attempt to break free from isolation:

> Would Clare have tried this too,
>   given the chance...
> Then listened? And when silence
>   came, said *John, alcoholic...*

The pamphlet's final Clare poem (dedicated to, and addressing, him) 'Remains' lists the unchanging aspects of life in Helpston that Clare would recognise if he returned home today:

> Still buildings you'd have known,
> still the buttercross,
> still thatch half a metre thick

This repetition is moving, covering village specifics alongside timeless activities: 'Still children running through snow'. The poem's closing stanza focuses on Clare's resting place with, I suggest, a faint play on Clare's imagery and reference to lying in grass in his last three lines of 'I Am':

> still dew settling on uncut grass,
> still your body,
> here, in its allotted ground.

The fourteen poems that don't refer directly to Clare explore pig farming and butchery, wild birds, flowers and animals, jobs, harvest, summer, and schooldays with a spare, lyrical intensity. While many of these subjects may be akin to Clare's poetic territory, Thompson proves himself to have a fresh, contemporary eye all his own. So, it's 'Welcome to the dialogue' for William Thompson: another voice joining John Clare in creative conversation.

Robert Hamberger

Joseph Skipsey, Selected Poems. Edited by R. K. R. THORNTON, CHRIS HARRISON and WILLIAM DANIEL McCUMISKEY. Third Edition, Revised and Extended. Newcastle upon Tyne: Rectory Press, 2024. Pp. 186. £10.00 (paperback).

Ten years ago I reviewed here a new selection of Joseph Skipsey's poems, edited by JCS Vice-President Kelsey Thornton, and W. D. McCumiskey, plus two CDs of Skipsey settings made by the poet's great-grandson, Chris Harrison (no. 35, 2016, p. 100). Skipsey, the Northumbrian 'Pitman Poet', was familiar to readers from Kelsey's article in the previous *Journal*, 'Joseph Skipsey and John Clare: Two Labouring-Class Poets' (no, 34, 2015, pp. 23-32), while Chris Harrison had entertained us at the 2015 Festival with his Skipsey settings. For this third edition of *Selected Poems* the three have combined their skills, resulting in a larger, richer edition, with more primary information on

Skipsey and his world (100 pages, now indexed, plus 100 pages of poems). Highly recommended.

John Goodridge

When It Rained for a Million Years. By PAUL FARLEY. London: Picador, 2025. Pp. 96. £12.99 (paperback).

In an ambitious poem, 'Close Reading', in Farley's new collection *When It Rained for a Million Years* (2025), Clare and Oliver Twist are imagined brushing past each other across time as they respectively flee from and flee towards what is now London. The two figures, Farley hypothesises, 'might have shared a pipe by a milestone', communing of their shared histories, the circumstances that had led to their fugitive frenzy. Oliver Twist, initially imagined in *The Mudfog Papers* as the resident of a murky, flat, vague Midland town delighted to welcome a conference of bores, only made sense in London. Conversely, Clare sprinted home, a beloved Mudfog.

 The poem puns on the much-butchered undergraduate activity of close reading, and also 'close' itself as a geographical marker, the two figures straddling fiction and reality to meet each other at a 'close'. The poem underlines the boundary-defying intricacy of this collection, an intricacy embodied in Farley's pervasively jaunty yet tightly-controlled formal structures. In these tercets, for example, 'milestone' looks to 'home', and the historical, geographical, and literary has endless personal resonances, with Farley clearly using this hallucinatory encounter as a cipher of his own gravitation towards and away from London. This hallucinatory, whimsical, but never unbounded energy is a constant in Farley's work.

 In his formal skill and clearly considerable ornithological knowledge, Farley is a more sarcastic, Liverpudlian Clare, and this collection exemplifies this sensibility. We don't have to look any further than 'Close Reading' to find this: Farley jazzily rhymes 'The Gandhi' with 'Sandy'. But if we do opt to look further, we will find a cornucopia of clever ornithological poems, emblazoned with Farley's trademark sardonic cheek, which has been perfected over decades. 'Swifts' is a truly clever poem, marauding us over the earth's skyline in time with the swift. The first stanza takes us from 'Brunelleschi's dome' to the 'campaniles of Rome', and before we know it we are in the glumly secular 'swing bridge at Preston Docks'. This is the 'only earth they know', scanning swiftly our various monuments, religious and industrial, which to the swifts are only an inconvenience. The speaker has always wanted to live life 'on the wing', invoking Romantic tropes, the weight of sublime stereotypes. By the end of the poem, we are forced out of swift-consciousness, with the speaker prosaically observing a 'frostbitten man (who's never seen snow)', who 'falls towards East Sheen'.

 Farley, a lifelong twitcher, seems, in poems like this, to have stumbled into a kind of divine realism, a learned desire to live on the ground. There are also wonderful poems that point out how birds are shaped by us, or how they could be like us. Farley is possibly the best poet in poetic tradition at expressing this rather simple truth, going beyond Clare in imagining birdsong as territorial bargaining, mundane courtship, and bureaucracy. In 'Wagtail Roost,

Cheshire Oaks, Outlet Village', the wagtails 'gather and huddle' in an improvised space constructed from our veneration of leisure. In 'The Workaround', Farley savagely points out that the simple parable of Bede's Sparrow is impossible with double-glazed windows: rather than a moment of warmth and solace, sparrows often simply die in contact with modern windows. And, in 'Turkeys', the gobbling of turkeys is imagined–once we crack the code–as turkeys voting for Christmas.

Crack the code we always must, and, once we do, the poems often open themselves up beautifully, as if an open sky lies enclosed between the words. This cleverness can sometimes be an obstacle, however, or can be a little redolent of Farley's influences. Poems like 'Three Rings', for example, sometimes seem a bit too reminiscent of Michael Donaghy and his obsession with invoking telecommunications as a metaphor for cognition, such as in 'The Excuse'. When Farley's speaker recalls 'let[ting] it ring three times / when drink dialling our old house', it could well be Donaghy's speaker recalling that, 'I pick up and there's no one there'. It seems sometimes like *The Mizzy* (2021) is a much finer collection, depicting the highs and lows of bird-watching and the sheer, childish excitement of hearing a mistle thrush sing in Liverpool, or seeing a goldcrest for the first time. Farley can be both ecological, elegant, and demotic; perhaps *The Mizzy* is a finer example of these elements being married. Certain poems in the collection, like 'My Last Drink', where the speaker finds himself imbibing a simple pint of lager, as always, sometimes seem a bit throwaway.

But this criticism is also a little unfair. The Donaghyesque poems also concern bereavement, and 'Three Rings' itself depicts absence, what it's like to not have the response you are so acclimatised to. The last stanza of this poem, knowing the emptiness of directories and exchanges, must contend with a 'dark / industrial building where love's never been / which isn't where I wanted this to land / and not what I want it to mean'. Farley dramatises the experience of writing about bereavement, and anyone who has lost a close family member knows exactly what he is wonderfully describing, the duel with nihilism, the coping in spite of the concrete realities that conjured a person. And some of the poems dedicated to wildlife are truly immersive, like 'Rewilding', a rollicking sonnet rhapsodising the beaver. Farley captures this creature in a scintillating fashion, commenting upon its 'assault on the vertical', and creates elaborate puns, such as stating idiomatically 'you need no introduction'.

I also loved 'Slush', which plays slushily with the conventions of poetry and contains a crystalline structure of puns and idioms as a panegyric to slush, an obviously innovative conception of a poem. Farley calls slush 'the bow wave of the glacier's creep that ploughs / earth and grit'. Farley's poetry itself, like slush, is fluid, pre-Socratic. If *The Mizzy* was for birders, this is a collection that more thoroughly and broadly grapples with the non-human but also with the human, with geology, and personal memory.

Sam Hickford

'Peasant Family Under the Trees' (1866), Hans Thoma. Harvard Art Museums/Fogg Museum, Bequest of Grenville L. Winthrop.

Contributors

EM CHALLINOR is a recent graduate of the University of St. Andrews. Their research interests include environmental anthropology, multispecies anthropology, and the anthropology of biological sciences. They have conducted research on the use of visual media and storytelling in anti-pollution activism, written on apocalyptic fiction for *Counterblast* magazine, and just transition and ethno-ornithology for *UnEarth* magazine.

EMLYN DAVID is a doctoral candidate at Université Bordeaux-Montaigne. In 2022, she wrote her MA dissertation 'Scenes of storytelling and the poetics of listening in the poetry of John Clare', which examines the forms and functions of storytelling in the poetry of John Clare. Her PhD research focuses on the representation of folklore and popular culture in nineteenth-century Scottish literature, more specifically in the works of James Hogg, George MacDonald and R. L. Stevenson. Other research interests include Romantic poetry, labouring-class poetry, Scottish literature and the representation of oral storytelling in the works of authors of the eighteenth and nineteenth centuries.

MARK FIDDES grew up along the Nene in Northamptonshire with a copy of *The Shepherd's Calendar* in his pocket. His sister is called Clare and he attended school next door to the asylum in which the poet spent his final years. Winner of 2024's Ledbury Poetry Competition, Mark's latest collection is *Other Saints Are Available* (Live Canon, 2021). Recent work has appeared in *The London Magazine*, *The Irish Times*, *The Madrid Review*, *The Little Review* and *Shearsman Magazine*. He has also been awarded the Oxford Brookes International Poetry Prize (2019) and The Ruskin Prize (2017) among others. He lives and works in the Middle East. <www.markfiddes.com>.

ROBERT HEYES is an inorganic chemist by training, a school teacher by profession, and a book collector by inclination. Over the years he has done a good deal of research on John Clare, with a particular emphasis on Clare's letters, and those of his friends and associates. Most recently, his essay 'John Clare and the Community of Naturalists' appeared in *The Cambridge Companion to John Clare* (2024). Robert's first essay in this journal 'John Clare and the Militia' was published forty years ago in 1985. Since then he has been one of the most prolific contributors to this journal in its history.

SAM HICKFORD has just completed a PhD at the University of St. Andrews on Clare and contemporary poetry in the British Isles. His poetry collection is entitled *Poems Sketched Upon the M60* (Littoral Press, 2021). Sam has published work in this journal previously and in *New Voices in Translation Studies*, and his wide-ranging journalism has been published in *The Guardian* and *The Tablet*.

CATHERINE MCNALLY is an MPhil student studying English at the University of Cambridge. Throughout her studies she has sustained an interest in the intersection between science and literature, which has inspired her current dissertation on William Blake's use of insects in his response to Isaac Newton. Her essay in this issue, an earlier version of which formed the final dissertation of her undergraduate degree, is her first publication. She is looking forward to making more contributions to scholarly discussion in the future.

CHARLOTTE STRAWBRIDGE's art features on this issue's front cover. She is a contemporary artist and writer, inspired by the flora and fauna of the British countryside, spirit animals and the 'peace of wild things'. She is drawn to oils for their playful, textural qualities, enjoying the spontaneity of painting *alla prima*. Charlotte completes most pieces in one session, aiming to capture the joy of a passing moment in nature. With each painting, she creates illustrated thoughts from the animal's perspective. These thoughts inspire contemplation on some big ideas, in gentle short stories. From lessons on mindfulness and gratitude, to observations on the little things and the joys of nature. <www.charlottestrawbridge.co.uk>.

Abbreviations

BIOGRAPHY *John Clare, A Biography*, Jonathan Bate (London: Picador, 2003)

BY HIMSELF *John Clare By Himself*, ed. Eric Robinson and David Powell (Ashington and Manchester: Mid-NAG and Carcanet, 1996)

COTTAGE TALES *John Clare, Cottage Tales*, ed. Eric Robinson, David Powell and P.M.S. Dawson (Ashington and Manchester: Mid-NAG and Carcanet, 1993)

CRITICAL HERITAGE *Clare: The Critical Heritage*, ed. Mark Storey (London: Routledge & Kegan Paul, 1973)

EARLY POEMS (I–II) *The Early Poems of John Clare*, ed. Eric Robinson, David Powell and Margaret Grainger (Oxford: Clarendon Press, 1989)

JOHN CLARE IN CONTEXT, ed. Hugh Haughton, Adam Phillips and Geoffrey Summerfield (Cambridge: Cambridge University Press, 1994)

JCSJ *The John Clare Society Journal* (1982–)

LATER POEMS (I–II) *The Later Poems of John Clare*, ed. Eric Robinson, David Powell and Margaret Grainger (Oxford: Clarendon Press, 1984)

LETTERS *The Letters of John Clare*, ed. Mark Storey (Oxford: Clarendon Press, 1985)

MIDDLE PERIOD (I–II) *John Clare, Poems of the Middle Period 1822–1837*, ed. Eric Robinson, David Powell and P.M.S. Dawson (Oxford: Clarendon Press, 1996); (III–IV) (1998); (V) (2003)

MIDSUMMER CUSHION *John Clare, The Midsummer Cushion*, ed. Kelsey Thornton and Anne Tibble (Ashington and Manchester: Mid-NAG and Carcanet, revised edition, 1990)

NATURAL HISTORY *The Natural History Prose Writings of John Clare*, ed. Margaret Grainger (Oxford: Clarendon Press, 1983)

NORTHBOROUGH SONNETS *John Clare, Northborough Sonnets*, ed. Eric Robinson, David Powell and P.M.S. Dawson (Ashington and Manchester: Mid-NAG and Carcanet, 1995)

PROSE *The Prose of John Clare*, ed. J.W. and Anne Tibble (London: Routledge & Kegan Paul, 1951, reprinted 1970)

SHEPHERD'S CALENDAR *John Clare, The Shepherd's Calendar*, ed. Eric Robinson, Geoffrey Summerfield and David Powell (Oxford: Oxford University Press, revised edition, 1993)